DOUBLE DECKER C.666

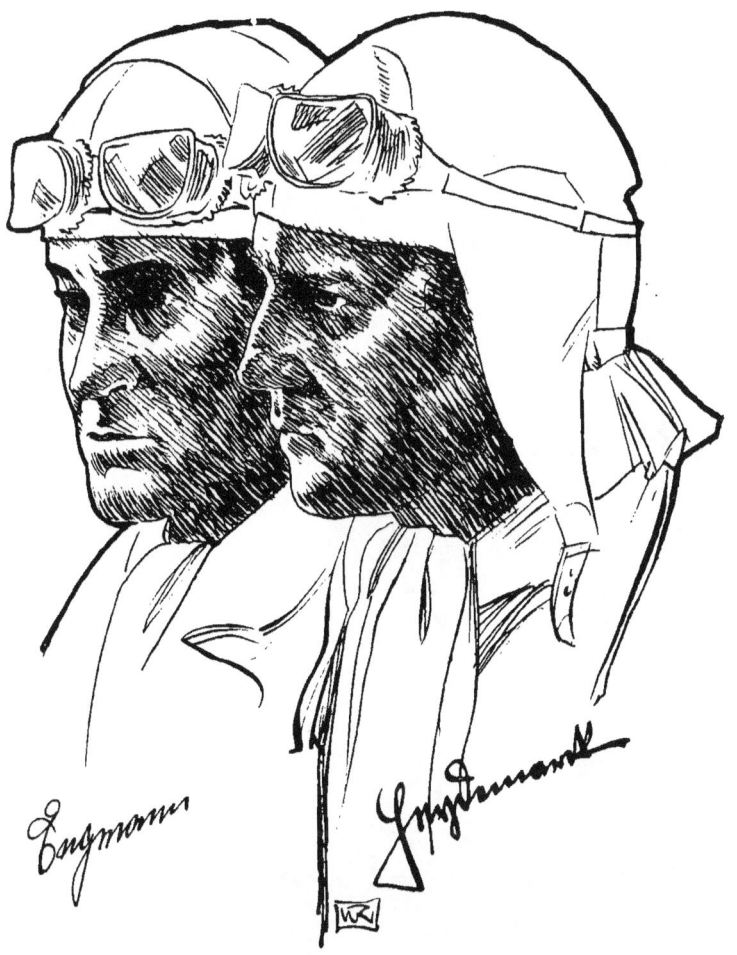

*Frontispiece*

# DOUBLE-DECKER C.666

**BY**
**HAUPT HEYDEMARCK**

TRANSLATED BY
CLAUD W. SYKES

The Naval & Military Press Ltd

*Published by*

**The Naval & Military Press Ltd**
Unit 5 Riverside, Brambleside
Bellbrook Industrial Estate
Uckfield, East Sussex
TN22 1QQ England

Tel: +44 (0)1825 749494

www.naval-military-press.com
www.nmarchive.com

*In reprinting in facsimile from the original, any imperfections are inevitably reproduced and the quality may fall short of modern type and cartographic standards.*

## CONTENTS

| CHAPTER | | PAGE |
|---|---|---|
| I. | A Chapter of Accidents | 1 |
| II. | Waiting for Orders | 7 |
| III. | Long Distance Reconnaissances | 10 |
| IV. | Through the Clouds | 33 |
| V. | IIII | 50 |
| VI. | Seeing it Through | 65 |
| VII. | Engine Trouble | 78 |
| VIII. | Thirty Degrees Below | 94 |
| IX. | Visiting Cards | 104 |
| X. | Save Me From My Friends | 118 |
| XI. | Anxious Moments | 133 |
| XII. | Night Swarms | 145 |
| XIII. | Bombing Epernay Station | 154 |
| XIV. | Into the Mist | 161 |
| XV. | "Cuckoo!" | 175 |
| XVI. | Whoso Diggeth a Pit for Others— | 186 |
| XVII. | I Had a Comrade—— | 203 |

## LIST OF ILLUSTRATIONS

"Take" Engmann and Captain Heyde-marck . . . . *Frontispiece*

| No. | | FACING PAGE |
|---|---|---|
| 1. | A French Dump | 24 |
| 2. | Above the Clouds | 46 |
| 3. | A Railway Bridge | 46 |
| 4. | Sidings for Armoured Trains | 50 |
| 5. | A Nieuport Climbing to Attack Us | 74 |
| 6. | Photograph of a Direct Hit on the "Pyramide" Camp | 76 |
| 7. | The French Aerodrome at Matougues | 88 |
| 8. | Trenches and No Man's Land | 92 |
| 9. | A Frost-bitten Hand | 126 |
| 10. | A French Camp in the Pinewoods | 100 |
| 11. | The Roads leading to the Camp revealed by Tracks in the Snow | 102 |
| 12. | German Aerodrome at Attigny | 126 |
| 13. | Flying over Ground-mist | 168 |
| 14. | "Take" Engmann in Action | 184 |
| 15. | Our forced Landing after a Fight in the Air | 200 |
| 16. | Engmann (left) before his last Flight | 206 |

I have no heroic deeds to report, but only our general experiences—I might almost say " Our daily bread ! "

I dedicate this book to my dear friend,
TAKE ENGMANN

HAUPT HEYDEMARCK,
*Captain (retired).*

# CHAPTER I

### A CHAPTER OF ACCIDENTS

IT was in the summer of 1912!
When we lieutenants of the 181st Infantry Regiment were assembled for the officers' gymnastic class, our commanding officer appeared and bade his adjutant read a regimental order.

" Progress in aviation—of vital importance for the army—junior officers required to train as pilots and observers—only voluntary applicants. . . . "

Colonel Morgenstern-Döring mustered us with a critical eye. " Does any gentleman want to apply ? " he inquired.

He had to laugh heartily when the whole class took an emphatic step forward.

" Very pleased to see such keenness," he said,

"but we must have a few officers left for the infantry."

. . . . .

We grew impatient when the replies to our applications failed to arrive in due course, but the regimental adjutant did his best to console us.

"Anyone who feels he can't wait," he announced one day, "can gain preliminary experience by participation in a balloon flight. The Chemnitz Aeronautical Association have sent us a free ticket. Who wants it?"

As all the youngsters wanted it, we had to draw lots. I had a piece of good luck—probably as compensation for the bad luck in love I was to experience later—and so won the ticket.

. . . .

With Lieutenant Roedel, of the "Crown-Prince" regiment, I travelled one day to Schwarzenberg. At the hydrogen factory there we were due to meet Professor Beuermann, of the Royal Technical School at Chemnitz, who was to take us up.

"I regret that it is impossible to start to-day, gentlemen," the professor greeted us, "there's an eighty kilometre an hour gale up aloft."

I laughed in what I then considered a superior fashion. "We'll travel quicker if that's the case," I remarked.

The professor shook his head. "And what about the landing?" he inquired.

I was bitterly disappointed, and begged him to try. But he smiled derisively; as an old hand he knew that my courage came from sheer ignorance of the danger and was in fact due to my imbecility.

"Very well, then, on your own responsibility," he said at last. He gave an order; the gas poured into the envelope with a hissing sound, and half an hour later the yellow ball of the balloon "Chemnitz" swayed above the wicker car.

The shelter from the wind that our starting-place enjoyed eliminated all danger from the ascent, so that my first experience of the upper air was pleasant enough. As the balloon's speed was equal to that of the air-current which carried it, we did not feel the wind or cold. I imagined myself the lord of the air, and was glad that I had insisted on going up. And as for the landing—well, Beuermann was an old hand who would bring us down safe and sound.

The gale drove us due east into Bohemia, so that I found it easy to locate our whereabouts, but after a trip of two hours, which I thoroughly enjoyed, we ran into snow clouds, and as our ballast was exhausted, we had to come down. The professor let the gas out of several valves; we dropped below the clouds and sighted land again. Our chances did not look particularly rosy when we saw that the gale was driving us towards a chain of three very long lakes.

Beuermann thrust his lower lip forward. "We must land at once, or this brutal cold will kill us."

He opened some more valves; the balloon began to fall quickly, and now we realized the perilous nature of the voyage upon which we had embarked so lightheartedly. When we viewed the landscape from a height of 1,000 metres, it looked to be gliding away slowly beneath us, but as we sank to a level barely above the trees, they seemed to rush past us at lightning speed. The gale had not abated, so that Beuermann was forced to land on hard, frozen snow, with a wind blowing at eighty kilometres an hour. There were bound to be some broken bones.

" Bend your knees sharply when we land," were the professor's final instructions.

The subsequent events took place so rapidly that we were barely conscious of them, but it was a lucky thing for us that we were travelling over fairly level ground. When we looked ahead, we saw that we were most unpleasantly near the first lake, so that something had to be done at once.

Beuermann pulled the line vigorously, tearing a big panel out of the envelope so as to let the gas out as quickly as possible. As the balloon had now lost all buoyancy, it was bound to remain on the ground—in theory, at least.

In our case, unfortunately, the business did not go off according to plan. The gale caught the empty envelope and whirled the car up aloft just as we were about to touch the ground. Then it let us flop down like a wet sack.

Down we went again at an alarming rate— now's the moment to bend your knees as Beuermann told you—and then—Bump! Bump! the car hit the ground with a resounding smack and turned over. Luckily it stuck where it was.

## A CHAPTER OF ACCIDENTS

We were thrown out, and for a few moments we all lay on the ground like squashed frogs. (See sketch at chapter heading.) Beuermann wiped the blood from his face; he had got a nasty knock from the heavy iron hoop that held the car-ropes. Roedel was kneeling and rubbing his left ankle.

I thought at first that I had been lucky enough to escape with a shaking and some bruises. With some difficulty I struggled up on my left leg and endeavoured to plant my right foot on the ground. But the right leg failed to respond to my will; it just hung limp, as if it had no connection with my body. It was most unpleasantly plain to me that I had broken my thigh; with a hollow laugh I resigned myself to the inevitable and subsided on to my back again. Damned bad luck!

My companions improvised a splint for my leg and eventually bedded me down on some straw in a peasant's cart; snowflakes fell gently as I was jolted over country roads to Gitschin. There my leg was set in a travelling splint, and on the following day I was sent by train to Chemnitz.

On the platform I was eyed with respectful curiosity, and rumours began to circulate.

"An officer wounded in a duel," was the general opinion. I began to feel I was a most interesting person.

. . . . . .

In the garrison hospital Dr. Petzsche pulled a long face. My right leg was quite ten centimetres shorter than my left.

"Goodbye to my uniform," I thought.

But he skilfully drew the splintered ends of bone apart by means of an expanding bandage, so that finally the leg was only three centimetres too short. As this disparity was counterbalanced by a falling of the other hip, I was able to remain in the army. Three months later I took my second trip in a balloon, but that time the landing went off beautifully.

## CHAPTER II

### WAITING FOR ORDERS

UNFORTUNATELY I was not yet fit for active service as an infantry officer when the order came to mobilize, but as in a moment of golden lightheartedness I had bought a thoroughbred I went off to the war in August, 1914, as adjutant to a Landwehr brigade. I had been compelled to abandon the idea of learning to fly until I was passed as completely fit again, and now, of course, I had no time to think of such things, because we had made up our minds to be home again when the autumn leaves were falling.

When the Champagne sector of the front became stabilized, our staff was quartered somewhere south of Moronvilliers, in a hollow only a few hundred metres behind the trenches, which was known as the " Witches' Kitchen."[1] As the telephone lines were usually shot away, my coal-black

[1] See the author's work, *Leuchtkugeln* (Starshells).

steed and I were responsible for the liaison with the division headquarters and the neighbouring brigade, and at night I was allowed to take part in patrol work. Lieutenant-General Count Vitzthum, my first chief, was killed by shrapnel fire, and Colonel Baron von Düring, his successor, fell a victim to a shell splinter. When the staff was moved back, and the war looked likely to last considerably longer than we had anticipated, I put in for a transfer to the Flying Corps.

In the summer of 1915 I was called up for training and underwent a short course of instruction in the Flying Schools at Gotha and Grossenhain. The following winter I was ordered to do a cross-country flight in association with another aeroplane, which I lost in a snowstorm. When I landed in Gotha, I saw a dark patch on the newly-fallen snow.

" What's up ? " I asked.

The commandant looked grave. " The other machine crashed on landing," he said. " Both occupants killed."

As the training courses had claimed a large number of victims, I was glad when shortly afterwards I was posted for active service and sent to Army Aviation Park, No. 3, at Rethel. That meant I was to fly over the ground in the Champagne sector where I had fought as an infantryman.

. . . .

We newly-fledged warbirds hung about the Park, eager for action, and waited to be called up. We seemed likely to kick our heels for a long time,

# WAITING FOR ORDERS

because the rainy autumn weather had curtailed flying activities very considerably, and consequently there were few casualties.

I was all on tenterhooks: to what department was I going to be posted? Was I to join the artillery flyers who directed the fire of the batteries by wireless? Or the Corps flyers who did the close reconnaissances? Or should I be detailed to one of the fighting squadrons that carried out the bombing operations? Or to H.Q. for long distance reconnaissances?

That appealed to me most of all, because it meant that under the conditions of trench warfare I should be called upon to do the work undertaken by cavalry patrols in open campaigns.

I found the uncertainty of my future activity quite thrilling.

. . . .

As an idle life did not suit me, I went out in the school machine piloted by Sergeant König, which was fitted with dual controls. After twenty-two flights I was allowed to handle the stick under his supervision.

I had "hunter's luck" with my first landing, for I put the machine down in the middle of a covey of partridges, three of which dashed themselves to death against the wires.

That seemed to break the spell. A few days later Captain Mohr applied for me for his squadron, No. 17, at Attigny. I had obtained my heart's desire: long distance reconnaissances.

## CHAPTER III

### LONG DISTANCE RECONNAISSANCES

FOR a month I flew with Sergeant Stattaus; then " Take " Engmann was allotted to me as pilot.

" How did you get that nickname ? " I asked.

Engmann laughed somewhat shamefacedly.

" Through my ignorance of mankind," he replied. " I read something in the paper about a foreign statesman called Take[1] and said to the other pilots : ' If I had a name like that, I'd go and get christened again.' From that moment onward they wouldn't call me anything but Take."

. . . . . .

" Herr Lieutenant ! "

Sleepily I make an effort to rise. Oh Lord, I'm on the dawn patrol to-day. I must hop out of bed !

[1] Engmann's namesake must have been the late Rumanian statesman, Take Jonescu.—TRANSLATOR'S NOTE.

## LONG DISTANCE RECONNAISSANCES

" What's the weather like ? "

My batman shrugs his shoulders. " There are some stars in the sky, sir, and some clouds as well."

I get up and slouch into the courtyard in my slippers. A clear sky, broken here and there by a few cloudlets. But the stars have not got that hard crystalline look of jewels set in the blue cloth of heaven ; they flicker uneasily like candle flames. That means the air is full of moisture, and clouds will come up in the early morning. But at present we have a clear sky, and we shall have to get a move on.

A quarter of an hour later I am in the messroom, where Engmann is waiting for me. An orderly brings steaming hot coffee—that tastes good ; bread and jam, and a boiled egg for each of us. Eggs are somewhat scarce, but by established tradition they remain the perquisites of the airmen detailed for dawn patrols. When I have eaten half a slice, I take a sly peep at Engmann ; munching away, he is just about to smear his third slice. He enjoys his breakfast.

To fill in time I pour myself out a second cup of coffee and sip at it until Engmann has swallowed his fourth and wipes his mouth with a contented air.

" Well, Take, come and have a look at the map now ! Orders for to-day : the usual long distance reconnaissance." I pass my right hand grandiosely over a space of 2,000 square kilometres on the map.

" Bombing objective : voluntary. Photography :

the railway lines at Châlons West Junction, the camp south of Bussy-le-Château, the aerodromes at Courtisols, Tilloy-Bellay and Auve."

" And how are we getting there ? " he asks.

I hand him the weather forecast. " Westerly winds—we'll go by Rheims."

. . . . .

A minute later our car rattles over the silent streets of Attigny. Engmann takes a look at the sky.

" I should say the wind will be south-west ; I can see swirls of cirrus clouds drifting north-east."

I admit that he is right.

" And we'll soon have a cloud-bank pushing up ; you can see the thick stuff coming along behind them."

We alight at the entrance to the aerodrome and walk up the cinderpath that leads to our hangar. A broad beam of light pours through the doorway and makes a sharply-cut patch on the path. I hail our two mechanics, Lance-corporals Schulz and Sievers.

" Good morning. You can clear off. No chance of going up at present."

Then I go over to the machine. " One minute, Take," I request, " I just want to put all my tackle right so that we can get off quickly if the weather's fit for flying later."

When I have done what is necessary and Engmann has had a look at the machine, we drive back into the little town.

. . . . .

# LONG DISTANCE RECONNAISSANCES 13

Arrived at my quarters, I lie down on my bed, fully dressed. "Wake me in an hour's time, Hugo," I tell my batman, "or earlier if the weather clears, even if it's only some sort of a hole in the clouds."

But I hardly seem to have dozed off when he wakes me up again.

"Six o'clock, sir, and it's raining a bit."

"Topping! Wake me up at seven." I turn over on to my left side and continue my nap.

. . . . .

6.20 a.m.

"Herr Lieutenant!"

"Hm?"

"There is a small break in the clouds."

Up I jump, and out into the courtyard again. Yes, look there—there's a lovely spot of blue sky. Ten minutes later Engmann and I are at the aerodrome.

"Well, there'll be something doing after all, Take. I'll ring up at once and find out what things are like at the front. Meanwhile you get the machine out."

When I emerge from the tiny guardroom, our crew have let down the hangar's door and are pushing the white bird out on to the green meadow. (See sketch at chapter heading.)

"Wind report is good," I announce. "Ten metres a second at 3,000, blowing north-west. So we'll gain height between Rethel and Attigny and fly over the front by Rheims."

, , , , ,

## DOUBLE-DECKER C.666

Half an hour after we have taken off I look at the altimeter which hangs above us in a position that allows us both to see it easily. The slim indicator points to 2,100 metres; I have only to fix up my camera; then we are ready to penetrate the enemy's lines.

I take the apparatus from its rack and consider the situation. Sunshine, with a slight haze: a yellow filter, an open lens and 1/250 of a second exposure are indicated. When I have made my arrangements, I signal Engmann to head for the front.

The roar of the engine renders conversation difficult. We have therefore agreed upon a simple code of signals, of which I will name only the most important.[1]

A whack on Engmann's right shoulder: right turn.

Whack on his left shoulder: left turn.

Rub his back between the shoulder blades: straight ahead.

Whack on his crash helmet: descend.

Wave with flat hand: enemy aircraft.

Opening fingers from clenched fist: enemy Archie.

If Engmann wants to draw my attention to anything, he sounds his throttle: Tirrp, tirrp, tirrp. If conversation is necessary, he has to cut his engine.

So I whack his left shoulder, and he goes into a left hand turn. " Hi-ee-ee ! " howl the bracing

[1] It was the usual arrangement in the German Flying Corps for the pilot to be an N.C.O., but the observer, as in the case of Double-Decker C.666, was a commissioned officer and in command of the machine.

# LONG DISTANCE RECONNAISSANCES

wires. When we have turned sufficiently, I polish his backbone with my hand: "Straight ahead, for the front!"

Slowly the aeroplane flattens out again. Five minutes later we pass the German trenches, and now we are over the French lines. The tension that has attacked our nerves during the flight to the front is now at its worst. When will the Archie fire their first shots, and where will they hit us?

Engmann fidgets on his seat above the tank, and leans out to right and left in his efforts to get a view beyond the engine. Likewise I twist my neck to gain a glimpse of the space ahead. I stand on tiptoe, holding on to the centre section, trying to look over the top of the upper planes. Why are there no shrapnel clouds?

If only the first of them would come along!

Slowly the trenches below glide away from us. From our height it seems an eternity before they disappear, and yet our flying speed is more than 120 kilometres an hour.

Still no Archie! No need to help my wary Take with whacks on the shoulders, because he knows perfectly well how to make things difficult for the gunners below. Even though there are as yet no shells to dodge, he has abandoned his straight course, and tacks at irregular intervals. He toes the rudder-bar quite gently so that we do not lose too much time with our zigzags.

If only that first shot would come! I give Engmann a nudge and endeavour to scan the expression on his face in the mirror before him.

I clench my fist and open it again, but he shakes his head; I repeat the signal, shrugging my shoulders:

"Still no Archie? What's up?"

Engmann answers with another shrug of the shoulders: "Wouldn't I like to know?"

Then: whoof!

The unholy row of a very near detonation makes us both flinch involuntarily, and at the same moment a blow from a gigantic fist seems to hit the floor of our machine, which shoots aloft as though propelled by a gust.

That is the first shot, and a damned good one too!

But in spite of its dangerous proximity, it is a welcome visitor, because it puts an end to our suspense. That significant little couplet of peace time:

" Almost half his life in arms
The soldier waits for war's alarms "

has a doubly bitter sound in an actual warfare.

Meanwhile Engmann has instinctively put the machine into a sharp right-hand turn, so that the second shell bursts far away to our left.

. . . .

Often the ranging of the enemy's shells and the zigzags by which we dodge them seem to me like a kind of aerial chess . . . an ingenious game, even though the stakes we play with are too high for us. But if our opponents want to claim them, they should not wait so long before beginning the

## LONG DISTANCE RECONNAISSANCES

match. If I know where they place their shells, I can make my countermoves. To-day, however, we are at a disadvantage, for when the first shot goes so near us, the following ones generally get a bit nearer still. If on the other hand the first is very wide of the mark, the gunner below becomes so flustered with the thought of the ticking off he will get that his marksmanship goes to pieces, and consequently he cannot get anywhere near us.

We can however, only take this sporting view of the business under two conditions: (1) We must not have a head wind against us that nails us to one particular spot and gives Archie too big an advantage, (2) we must not be too far behind the enemy's front to get home in a glide if our engine is hit. Although we seldom get a combination of both these conditions on long distance reconnaissances, I prefer—or, more correctly, I dislike less—being potted in the air to being peppered in the trenches, because up aloft I have the power of action; I do not just have to stick it out. Down below I am a miserable worm that must burrow in the earth, and although no one aims directly at me, mines and shells rend the soil that protects me—and are likely to rend me too. Up above I am a mark for the gunners. But I am a free bird that does not need to crouch motionless; I can employ the wiles of a hunted animal to wriggle my way through the narrow meshes of the net of steel splinters and leaden bullets that is set for me. Moreover my attacks of the " cold feet," to which we all are prone, are not so severe, because the roar of the engine makes the bursting shells sound far less dangerous than they really are.

. . . . .

We do not remain long in the new course we have taken because we do not want to give Archie our range again.

Half-left turn!

We'll see where their next shell bursts. Ah, there it is already! A couple of hundred metres behind us on the left a little white cloud takes shape in the air—bigger and bigger it grows—and at last the sharp report reaches our ears. And there's another! They look like lumps of cotton-wool—quite pretty little things—but masters of our fate, perhaps. A jagged piece of shell in your body, or a shrapnel bullet through your head—and it's the finish! But we only think about such things afterwards; up aloft we have no time to worry about them.

Almost imperceptibly we shift to our right.

Now the officer doing the spotting for Archie thinks he has got our range more or less and sends a quick series of shells and shrapnels after us. But we fly faster than he can correct the errors, and so those little clouds are always behind us. Fainter and fainter grow the sounds of their explosions in our ears—and at last we cease to hear them.

Straight ahead now!

Whoof! Whoof!

Two shells in front of us. A couple of seconds later a cloud of white smoke swishes in between our interplane struts. Oh, hell! What a stink of burnt-out gases, and with them comes the unpleasant realization that the blighter has got our height perfectly. Engmann puts the machine's nose down and dives; though we lose height, we gain speed. We can risk it; at 3,000 metres the loss of a few hundred cannot make much difference.

That was the correct move; the next cloud appears high above us, to our right. Capital! So now we even out again so as not to drop too low. And bear a bit to the right—yes—that's good.

But now they've spotted our little dive. Whoof! Whoof! To right and left of us simultaneously; that's mean!—very mean! Seems to be a battery of four guns that wasn't there before, and *M. le capitaine* who commands it is a hell of a smart fellow. Good for him—and so much the worse for us. Our change of altitude has not availed.

Damn the blighter, he's a blasted good shot!

Whoof! Whoof! one quite close, to our left, another farther away, behind us. And both a bit lower; he has certainly spotted our loss of height.

Hoo-ee-ee-ee! Hoo-ee!

He's lucky with his shrapnels, too, for a metallic clang on the left plane makes me turn my head. Apparently a bullet has hit a bracing wire or a strut. Yes, there it is; I can see two round holes in the fabric. The wind from the propeller tears at their frayed edges.

It is high time for us to get out of this witches'

kitchen. I can see the smoke trails of the shrapnels stretching out to mark the direction of the shots ... they make the observer's task easier, but help us too because they enable me to locate the position of the battery that fired them.

Biff! Engmann gets a hefty whack on his left shoulder : sharp left turn !

We shoot off almost at a right angle from our old course, and our tactics are at once successful, for the next ten or twelve shots burst harmlessly far behind us. Then follows a slight pause. The enemy down below has got to do a bit of hard work ; new measurements—new tables—new calculations—new sighting—before he can fire again.

Where is he likely to plant his next shots? Breathless seconds pass ; at length they come, but this time they are far too short. They continue to burst behind us, and at last they cease.

A curious picture—the airway we have flown is plastered with cloudlets—more than a hundred of them. The latest arrivals gleam silvery-white in the sunshine, while the older ones lose their compactness and begin to fade away into the blue heaven. The early morning breeze tosses them hither and thither, pulling them to pieces until I can hardly see a trace of them left.

Farther and farther we push our way into the enemy's land.

The white lines of the communication trenches disappear in woods or sink into hollows ; then the big camps that contain the reserves make their

# LONG DISTANCE RECONNAISSANCES

appearance. The first of them are dug out of the ground, for they are still within the range of our artillery, but farther back there are barracks of wood and sheet iron. Excellent targets for bombs. Through the green of the pine and fir woods the white chalk gleams traitorously where the soil has been turned up, revealing yet further buildings to my eye.

Wherever the traffic—relief and munition—columns, transports of materials, field kitchens—has been crowded together at the approaches to bridges or villages, the grass at the side of the roads is worn away.

Now we are flying alongside the railway lines.

The first station that we fly past is the railhead for the daily traffic. There are huge sidings to be seen, a network of new lines, rows of sheds and stores, and suddenly, far away to southward, I espy a thin trail of smoke. I pick up my glasses and examine it. The vibration of the engine makes the landscape dance up and down madly in the round lenses, so that I have to hold the binoculars jammed against my goggles, but at last I focus on the train. I can count all its trucks; there are twenty-one of them, most of which are covered in. I look at the chronometer; 8.35 a.m. I bend down to the railway map affixed on the board in front of me and record my observation on it.

Then follows an incident that gives me food for mirth. The engine-driver has seen the *avion boche* and strives to camouflage his train by blowing off clouds of smoke and steam. But all the same we spot you through it, old boy. Don't worry, however, we're not going to hurt you, so just carry on!

Then I search the roads with my glasses. Nothing much doing to-day. I can see a car tearing along the road to Châlons; behind it a mighty column of dust rises into the air and spreads over the fields between which the road runs. The car overtakes a column of ten or twelve lorries that also seem in a devil of a hurry; perhaps the German machine overhead makes them nervous; they are afraid of its bombs. Don't be alarmed, *messieurs*.

Beyond the wood there is an aerodrome in the neighbourhood of the Ferme de Metz. It is occupied by Escadrille C28. The brown hangars and grey tents stand out sharply against the green meadow, where there is a white landing-sign, laid out in a T shape, just like ours. A Caudron is about to start—a nice little machine. I scan the aerodrome again through my glasses and discover that there are six hangars. Formerly there were only four; that means reinforcements. Quickly I extract the camera from its rack. Everything is ready—withdraw the shutter from the plate—grip the handle with the left hand—finger of right hand on the release—press camera firmly against my chest—focus objective—click!—photo taken—change plates—re-wind focal plane—put camera back—job done.

Then, holding on to the centre section, I lean

# LONG DISTANCE RECONNAISSANCES 23

overboard and survey the air above and below me and to right and left in search of hostile aircraft. There is only one effective means of defence against this worst of all perils, and that is—don't be caught napping!

The landscape below me is strewn with long sheds. The heavy traffic and the width of the roads tell me that here is a dump. (See Illustration No. 1.)

This neighbourhood is thickly strewn with aerodromes. To the south of Bouy village another looms into sight. I am just about to put down my glasses when a little speck runs across the field of vision. I try to focus on it, but it eludes me. I put the glasses down quickly. Now where was that speck? Ah, yes, over there—I see her—an old Farman. Well, she's nothing to worry about, and in any case she's only 800 metres up. Quite likely she hasn't seen us yet as we are so high above her; she's heading straight for the front to do a bit of spotting for the French artillery.

Well, let her go!

We proceed; Châlons-sur-Marne station comes into sight. The most important railway junction for the army corps facing ours. Here is the destination of all the trains that carry troops, munitions, provisions and all the hundred and one other things that an army needs. New lines are continually being laid down, new sheds grow out of the soil like mushrooms, new sidings make their appearance, new platforms are in process of building.

Slowly the town and station glide towards us. I see long rows of trucks; a goods train, comprising fifty of them, is just about to leave, while smoke issues from the funnels of three other engines that are waiting with steam up. I note the extent of the traffic on my map and reach for the camera.

Whoof!

Half left ahead of us the first shell bursts. Of course there are Archies here—a whole battery of them.

Can't be helped; we must wing our way into the witches' kitchen, for I have orders to take a series of vertical sectional pictures of the station. As my photos must overlap each other, it is no good trying to get slanting views; I shall have to fly right over the station.

Archie is not the worst of our troubles, although just the tiniest splinter of a shell in our engine here—thirty kilometres behind the front—would entail most serious consequences. Even if they do not hit us, they betray us, for they scream a message to every French machine in the air anywhere within a ten kilometres radius: "A Boche is here; come along and down him!" And we know from prisoners that the Nieuport squadron, No. 64, at St. Etienne-au-Temple Aerodrome, is specially detailed to look out for those pestilential lone flyers of our No. 17 that appear over Châlons day by day with mathematical precision—once, twice, thrice a day. The Nieuports will be put on our track by the pretty little clouds that Archie sends up after us, but it can't be helped; we must carry on.

To-day Archie put a concentric fire on us

I  A FRENCH DUMP

*Facing page* 24

# LONG DISTANCE RECONNAISSANCES

as soon as we were over the town. It is doubly unpleasant because this time we have such a limited space to dodge them in; to get my sectional pictures I am compelled to fly vertically over the station and follow the direction of the lines. I whack Engmann into the right course and take my photos, flying in the circle of the barrage which rages around us like a hurricane of iron, lead, fire, and smoke. From below it must look as if our machine is being riddled with bullets and torn to shreds by shell splinters, but when I have finished the job and give Engmann a whack to indicate that he can fly north-east and take us out of this hot corner I am joyfully surprised to discover that we have not sustained a single hit. I laugh to myself; not every bullet has its billet.

A few minutes later the last smoke of bursting shells is far behind us, and shortly afterwards we are rewarded for the noble way in which we stuck it.

Hitherto we have had a clear view of the sky and landscape, but now come scraps of clouds that we can use as cover. But there's a reverse side to the medal; in the layer of stratus[1] that is in process of formation I can see large-sized cumuli[2] floating, the upper edges of which I place at about 4,500 metres, while we are flying at 4,000.

Consequences: We are exposed to unpleasant

---

[1] The stratus cloud is formed of mists and fogs that make their appearance in the bottoms of valleys and over low-lying ground on calm evenings and subsequently spread upwards over the surrounding country like an inundation.

[2] The cumulus is the name applied to those convex or conical heaps of clouds which increase upwards from a horizontal base.

surprises from Nieuports which can make good use of each cover. We shall have to keep our eyes trebly skinned, and meanwhile I must go on combing the landscape.

Almost immediately I see something worthy of note. Thirty huge columns of dust are floating along the main road from Châlons to Suippes. A column of lorries. I quickly mark its location and time in the map.

South of a large village I see a number of circles: riding-school rings. Cavalry quartered there; no sign of any motor transport. To northward of the village long wooden buildings, the roofs of which are camouflaged with pine branches so as to give the appearance of a wood to aircraft flying overhead. Those are the stables. They would be a good mark for any steel arrows. I consider the matter; sidewind—that means I must bear slightly to the left. Speed: present speed will do, if I am a bit ahead of the mark. Yes, we're about right now! I empty the box slowly so as to make the missiles spread out; then I shall hit something, at least. The bright steel darts gleam in the sunshine as they fall.

As we fly close to a high tower of clouds, Engmann suddenly sounds his throttle.

Tirrp! Tirrp! Tirrp! The next moment he points skywards. "A Frenchie!"

I jerk my head up. Yes, there's a Nieuport not twenty metres over our heads, just coming out of the edge of the clouds. Wings and cockpit are painted light blue, and the red, white and blue

## LONG DISTANCE RECONNAISSANCES 27

cockades gleam like two gigantic butterfly's eyes. At such close distance all the details of the machine appear larger than they really are. (See illustration on jacket.)

"Sorry—false move, *mon vieux*." He must turn away before he can dive on us because he was directly above our heads when he emerged from the clouds. But before he can execute this manœuvre, I swing my machine gun round and pepper him with a short, sharp series. He promptly goes into a steep turn and heads for the clouds again. But just as I am rejoicing at his discomforture, I get a second nasty shock.

Tack—tack—tack—tack—tack rattles a machine gun in my left ear. I swing my own weapon round again. Ah, there's another Frenchman! And—damn it all—a third a bit behind him! Well, No. 3 is not dangerous for the moment, but I must take care he doesn't spring some surprise on me later. No. 2, however, is uncomfortably near; I must tackle him first. I sight him carefully; that's all right! Then I open fire on him. He appears to be unpleasantly shocked by my alertness. Perhaps he has shot away a drum of ammunition or his gun has jammed; at any rate he puts his machine into a steep right hand turn. Then I look round quickly; I must not lose sight of the other two. No fear of that, for both are at hand. No. 3 is diving on to my tail from behind, while at the same time No. 1 is slanting down on me from the right.

This last is the nearer and demands my

immediate attention. I let him fly into my sights and then send twelve shots in his direction. A short pause. Then another twelve. That appears to damp his ardour somewhat, for he sweeps round in a wide circle and hangs on to his colleague's tail. But even so I get no satisfaction out of the business because the next moment a burst comes rattling down on me from above. Without a second's delay I swing my gun round and answer his fire. Take careful aim—twelve shots—eyes open—finger pointed—short pause—aim again—and shoot. Always remember to be as economical as possible with ammunition.

Wonderful how calm one is ! No trace of excitement ; my heart is beating quite normally.

I give my assailant a third and fourth series of twelve, but he shows no signs of relinquishing his attack. A smart fellow—I must give him his due credit.

Now barely a hundred metres separate our machines.

Good old Take is doing his share splendidly. As soon as he hears me stop shooting, he puts the machine into another turn of the zigzag he is making. I have to grin when I think what a lot of trouble he is giving that stout fellow who sticks to us like a leech ; our tactics never let him get a steady shot at us.

Just as I have him sighted again and am about to press the trigger-button, a metallic clang mingles with the rattle of his machine gun. Ah ha, a hit !

This time I fire off a longer series ; thirty

# LONG DISTANCE RECONNAISSANCES

shots. And—hurrah!—suddenly my hunter rolls over on his left wing—his machine goes on to its nose and down in a vertical dive. Got him! Ah!

The next Frenchman has approached to within 200 metres of us, but as soon as he sees what has happened he goes into a steep turn, and remains at a respectful distance. So does the third.

Suddenly: "Whoof!"; the first shell from the Suippes Archie. It burst half-way between us and our two opponents. That feeds them up; they put their machines about and make off in a southerly direction.

I sign to Engmann to throttle his engine, and tell him the good news so that he can rejoice with me.

"And now for the bombs!"

Through his goggles my good Take gives me a look of horror. He does not need to speak; I can read his thoughts; "If we had got a bullet in one of their detonators just now——"

For that very reason we are under orders to throw our dangerous "eggs" overboard before going into action. But when a fight is suddenly sprung on us, as to-day, one has no time to do it.

I whack Engmann into an easterly course, where we shall find some promising objectives. After the hot fight in the air we do not feel particularly impressed by the shells and shrapnel that Archie sends after us.

As I look around for an objective my eye is attracted by the captive balloon at Layal, which has been hauled down and lies in its nest on the ground. What about it? I could do the job better if only I had a sack full of " flying mice "[1] instead of my two twenty-kilo bombs. But unfortunately we are no longer supplied with those pretty little toys. They were such jolly things!

I take the pin out of the detonator, release the safety catch on the racks and free the lever. When I have signalled Engmann to fly against the wind towards my objective, I get the balloon into my sights. Good, that's the right angle.

" Bump! bump! "

I despatch the two explosive bombs on their downward journey, and a few seconds later I send the incendiary bomb after them. Then I lean over the cockpit to watch the progress of my missiles. Smaller and smaller they grow as they whizz down, and very soon I can no longer distinguish them. As we are at a height of 3,000 metres, a quick half-minute will see them down to the ground.

They are at their journey's end now. And look—both the explosive fellows drop quite close to the balloon. Although neither makes a direct hit, I am at least pleasantly sure that the flying splinters will perforate the balloon's envelope. And how about the incendiary bomb? It has not realised expectations, for I see that it has gone down behind the inflating apparatus. What a pity! No, only half a pity, for now I see it has hit a shed which is easily recognizable despite its camouflage of pine-branches. Thick smoke belches out of it.

[1] Small bombs, about the size of a hand-grenade.

## LONG DISTANCE RECONNAISSANCES

Something accomplished, at any rate! I point out the hit to my good Take, who responds with a joyous grin. Then I whack him on the shoulder, and he heads for the front again.

When we have wormed our way through the barrage Archie puts up, we whirl over the trenches. Homeward bound, at last!

A sense of relief flows through our limbs. How beautiful the earth looks! There is the valley with the river winding through its meadows and villages. There is the canal with its poplars that cast their long shadows over the fields when the morning sun shines.

Engmann throttles down a couple of pegs, and we glide slowly earthwards at 800 revs. That is the proper way to do it, because our eardrums are still acclimatized to the rarefied atmosphere of the upper regions; as the air thickens with our descent, the strain caused by the unwonted pressure increases. The contrast is so great when we make a quick descent that it sets our heads humming like a well-populated beehive. Even when we glide slowly down, we have to open our mouths and inhale vigorously, pumping the air against the eardrums.

A quarter of an hour after we have passed the trenches, we make a good landing on our own aerodrome.

. . . . . .

When we have rolled up to our hangar, my chief comes out of his little hut and shakes our hands.

" Well ? " he inquires.

I report myself home from a long distance reconnaissance with the words "Nothing particular."

Then I show him my map.

"Railway traffic slight." Conning my entries, I give him its details. "Activities at stations normal. Aerodrome . . ." I count the number of aerodromes noted on my map. "Photography: Ferme de Metz aerodrome and sectional photos of Châlons railway stations. Enemy aeroplanes . . ." I give a brief description of my fight in the air. "Archie: very hot behind the French lines and round about Châlons, otherwise nothing to make a song about." Meanwhile Engmann has been inspecting the bus with the mechanics.

"Machine hit twice by Archie, and four times in the fight. One bullet through the left front strut."

Captain Mohr nods. "Good; thanks. Please write out your report at once so that I can pass it on to H.Q."

"Very good, sir."

. . . . .

When the holes have been repaired, it is customary to put rings round the patches, with the dates of the fights in which the damage was done. Holes made by machine guns are marked with red rings, but hits from Archie only have thin black ones round them.

I go up in the esteem of my two mechanics with every new hole they find in my machine when I come home, but I certainly do not share their opinions on this point.

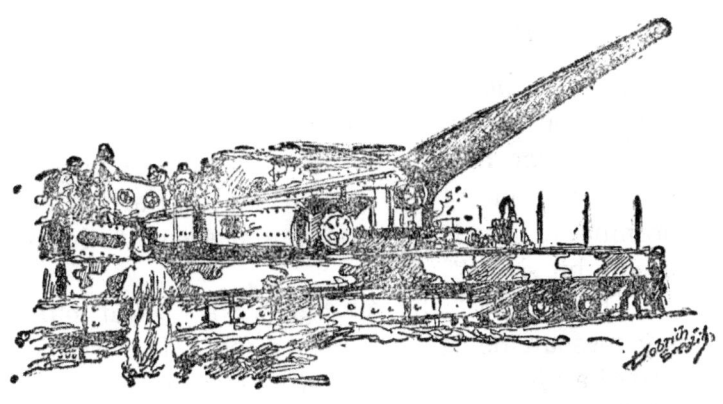

## CHAPTER IV

### THROUGH THE CLOUDS

NEARLY a whole week of rain, but to-day the sun is shining . . . fleetingly, through holes in the clouds.

"Well, Take, I think we'll have a try at all events. It's three times twenty-four hours since we last saw a Frenchie, so there's bound to be something new on. Besides H.Q. are howling for a photo of the railway bridge north-west of Châlons."

Engmann nodded.

"I've ordered the machine out," he informed me.

"Good. Then I'll go and inquire from 'froggy'[1] about the weather prospects."

---

[1] Froggy = Laubfrosch, slang term for the Field Meteorological Station. Derived from the German habit of keeping a frog in a jar as a weather prophet.—TRANSLATOR'S NOTE.

I went to the telephone. " Here Field Meteorological Station " came the reply.

" Good morning. Can you tell me the height of the bottom of the cloud bank. Early this morning it stood at 1,300, but it seems to have lifted a bit since."

" That's right," the voice growled. " Our midday measurements give it as 2,500. The wind's shifted a bit, too. Now blowing strong south."

" Thanks. Ring off."

. . . . .

When I went for Engmann with the car at twelve, noon, he looked at me inquiringly.

" What about a meal first ? "

" A meal ? And then go and get a bullet in our full tummies ? You know perfectly well we can only take the risk when they're empty."

Everything was ready for us except the camera. Yes, of course, it was Sunday !—a free afternoon for everyone, except the Flying Corps. At last the photographic orderly came slinkering along, but without the camera. When he saw my expectant attitude, he broke into a mild trot.

" All three cameras are being repaired," he announced.

That had never happened before, and it was particularly annoying to-day, because H.Q. wanted that photo. He launched out into a longwinded explanation, but I cut him short.

" I'm not interested in how you wangle it, but I've got to have a serviceable camera somehow."

Then I joined Take in the machine. " We'll

land in the park," I said. "We'll have to borrow a reserve camera there."

Take, who had been kneeling on his seat in order to listen to me ticking the man off, now settled himself down preparatory to taxying off. The next moment he turned to me with a sorrowful face and pointed to the manometer.[1] I craned forward, full of curiosity, and saw that its indicator stood at zero.

"Well, use your pump, man."

Engmann made a dozen strokes with the hand pump, but the indicator refused to budge.

"Pressure valve blowing off," he announced.

Consequently he had cause to repent at his glee over the ticking off I gave the photographic orderly, for now the weight of my wrath descended upon him. Fortunately our two mechanics repaired the trifling damage in a few minutes after they had likewise come in for a share of the rough edge of my tongue.

When the pressure on the main tank was steady, we set out on the flight which had begun so ominously. Fifteen minutes later we landed in Rethel, where we found Captain Rosenthal, the deputy O.C. Park, as helpful as usual. He ran himself nearly off his legs to satisfy our demand, but unfortunately the peace of Sunday afternoon reigned in his domain. The quarters of the photographic section were closed, and the staff were making holiday somewhere in the little town. We chased after them in a car, and were

[1] The manometer registers the pressure on the main benzine tank.

lucky enough to find the storekeeper, so that we were able to take off exactly an hour after we had landed.

"Many thanks!"

"*Hals- und Beinbruch!*"[1]

. . . . .

To make up for lost time we take the shortest way to the front, via Massiges. We ought to be able to reach 2,500 metres before we cross the trenches. The air is a bit tricky to-day, but with a powerful engine like ours, that does not matter much. The strength of our 160 horses will pull us safely through all airpockets and swirls.

I look up; overhead the clouds are scudding fast. Between them blue patches of sky make fleeting appearances. And every time we leave the sunlight and enter the shadow of a cloud, bump! a gust gets hold of our bird, and Engmann has to pull and push his controls to flatten her out again.

Two thousand metres at last. Below and ahead of me gleam the white lines of the trenches. I peer overboard. Funny: we seem to be moving jolly quickly. Of course it's a gust; it gets its strong shoulders under our bird and gives it a shove—forward and upward—only to let us down with another bump. And as we drop, I see that our speedy progress was only an illusion, for now

[1] There is no adequate English rendering for this expression, the literal meaning of which is "neck and leg breakage." Like all other flying men, the German aviators at the front had their own superstitions, one of which was that it was a fatal proceeding to wish a flyer "good luck" at the beginning of a trip. If, however, someone expressed the hope that he might break his legs and his neck, he felt certain that he would come back safe and sound.—TRANSLATOR'S NOTE.

it almost looks as if we are being driven backwards. But that is another illusion. In reality we are pushing our way forwards ... slowly but surely.

Our height is 2,400 metres when we reach the German trenches. I whistle to myself softly. We are going to have a lovely time with Archie to-day, for if we fly below the clouds, they will form a background against which our machine will be sharply silhouetted; moreover the gunners will know perfectly well that we cannot be flying higher than the underneath surface of the clouds, of which they will have the measurements. It is lucky for us that those clouds do not form an even bank; clumps of them sag below the general level and can be used by us to hide in when we seek concealment from the telescopes and measuring instruments of the gunners. Also we can dodge in and out of the main cloudbank at intervals. We have tried that trick before, however, and made the discovery that it is easier to bring off in theory than in actual practice.

Or shall we push our way through one of the many holes in the cloudbank and climb to 3,000 metres before crossing the lines? Engmann gives a snort with his throttle and endeavours to read my facial expression in his mirror. " What shall I do? " ask the shrugs of his shoulders.

I point upwards with my hand. " We'll get above the clouds right away."

He nods and pulls his stick towards him.

We look upwards anxiously, hoping to find the entrance to one of those holes through which shines the firmament of heaven. The sky has such a strong tint to-day—like a bold splodge of Prussian blue on an artist's palette.

My gaze turns southward. In the direction of the Marne I see many more blue patches sailing along between the shreds of cloud. And farther away the sky seems absolutely cloudless. Topping! We'll be able to do our reconnaissance work all the better when we get there. Right on the farthest horizon there are more clouds, forming fantastic towers that might belong to castles in fairyland.

We are now quite close to the lower rim of the clouds. Delicate tissues of cloud fabric whirl past us at lightning speed. Here comes a blue hole—quickly followed by a dense blanket—now we are bathed in the sun's gold—and the next moment we see the sky only through a thick veil. But at least we can see it.

When the next gap comes, we shall continue our search for the " blue hole." A detestable business!

" Hi-e-e-e-e ! " whistle the bracing wires as the bus goes into a steep right-hand turn ; we are going to screw our way up through this big gap. And—it looks as if we shall manage it all right.

Appearances are deceptive. Suddenly the blue sky is washed away, as if with a wet sponge. We cannot find it again, and all at once we are bang in the middle of the cloud-mist.

Well, that's not so serious. In a few seconds—or a few minutes, at the latest—we shall bore our way through the layer and come out above it.

# THROUGH THE CLOUDS

I lean overboard. Ah, there's the earth again! If only that beloved vision would abide with us! Flying through thick clouds is the most fearsome business I can ever imagine. After a little while one loses all sense of equilibrium; one's judgment is only reliable when the eye can hold fast to some fixed point that creates a feeling of balance. In our case it does not matter whether this point is on the ground below us, in the air beside us or in the sky above.

Experiments in Berlin have proved the truth of my assertion. The subject is blindfolded and strapped in a chair, which can be tipped, tilted or reversed by a special apparatus. After a few rotations in all directions the machine is stopped, whereupon the poor fellow in the chair is asked to say whether his feet are pointing earthwards or whether he is lying on his back or standing on his head. The report concludes with these words: " Hardly one subject was able to give an accurate answer."

It is true that ingenious implements have been devised to tell the pilot the cants of his long and traverse axes. But they do not seem to function accurately; only a few days ago they did not prevent one of our biggest aeroplanes from crashing in a fog, so that the crew were burnt to death.

Meanwhile Engmann is still climbing.

Good Lord! the earth has disappeared again. I look upward. Shine forth, sun!

Then I cast a hasty glance at the compass, because we have to keep on steering due south, whether we are in or above the clouds. At present both of us confident. Our last farewell view of the earth which is now veiled from us gave us a sense of balance, which we still retain. But our hopes and fears turn the next few seconds into long-drawn hours.

At last the sun breaks through the clouds again ; it is as pale as the moon's disc, but to us it is a symbol of hope. Now we shan't be long in these clouds !

But our hopes were too previous. A few seconds later whirling wraiths of mist swallow up all the sun's faint rays again. I glance at the compass—the glass is covered with fog. I find a bit of waste and wipe the moisture away. In a few moments another layer of drops has veiled the needle once more.

No, this sort of thing can't go on ! We simply cannot stand this ghastly reeling about in the void indefinitely.

Once again the sun's pale orb appears through the cloud. But the last time we saw it, it was straight ahead of us, and now it shines down on us from behind and on our left. That means we have completely lost our direction.

Before I can signal Engmann into our proper course, the fog swallows us up once more.

My goggles are full of moisture on their inner sides. I push them up on my forehead to regain my sight. But I can only peep out through the merest gap in my eyelids, for the cold wind from the propeller whistles cuttingly.

Will the sun never come back?

If only I could get just the tiniest glimpse of earth—for a couple of seconds. I lean overboard and strive to pierce the dark grey masses below me. In vain!

Then I jerk my head upwards. Was that not a ray of light just now? No—not the faintest gleam —not yet!

And now the last vestige of my sense of balance disappears. I grip a strut with either hand and stare at the rev.-counter. If its indicator now began to drop slowly, it would mean that things were serious.

The altimeter shows a height of 3,000 metres; we have therefore climbed 500 metres in the clouds. But the bank can't be as big as all that; I should have given it a height of 200 metres—not more. There is only one possible explanation— we have blundered into the clouds at a spot where a tower of them rises above the average level of the bank.

When shall we be delivered from our intolerable suspense?

To be crashed by treacherous clouds—oh Lord!

It seems to me as if our engine's iron song were not so clear as usual. It does not relish swallowing the cold, damp air about us, and the thick fog muffles its notes.

Three thousand one hundred—says the altimeter.

And still no kindly ray to lighten our darkness! I crouch down on my seat. Ought I to strap myself in so as to avoid being thrown out of the cockpit if we roll over on one or other wing? I consider the matter; even if the machine were to turn turtle, there is always the chance that she would catch herself after we had dropped a couple of hundred metres. It would not necessarily mean a crash.

I quickly seize the ends of the belt that hang down on either side of me and buckle them to.

Then suddenly a strange sensation sets my body all a-quiver. We are flying sideways—we are no longer on an even keel—we are sideslipping! If the sun does not come soon, it is all up with us.

Acting under the impulse of a sudden decision I unbuckle the belt again, lean over and whack Engmann three—four times on his crash-helmet. Down! down!

My signal is a relief to good old Take, who pushes the stick over with exorbitant energy and puts the machine into a nose-dive. He cuts his engine—we are gliding. Wonderful!

Now our danger is lessened because we can put more trust in the rev.-counter. But when I try to nod to Engmann in the mirror, I find the glass coated over with fog.

Down and down we glide. The slim indicator of the altimeter continues to fall.

3,000—2,900—2,800—2,700—2,600.

We ought to be able to see the earth soon!

2,500!

And—miracle of miracles!—the last veil is torn asunder—there lies the earth! Lies—did I say? No, it hangs, and most crookedly, too!

## THROUGH THE CLOUDS

Or rather—we hang down badly over our right wing. Instinctively Engmann pushes the stick to the left, and slowly our bird regains her horizontal level.

Both of us are filled with wonderful, overwhelming joy! I look down; we are only just over the French reserve positions. I nudge Engmann and show him where we are. We both laugh heartily when we think how we have been tossed about in the clouds.

"It doesn't matter now," I reflect, "we'll try how we can get along underneath the clouds. Far better risk a peppering from the French shrapnel than go on indefinitely tumbling about in that fearful void of a cloudbank!"

Keenly I search the ground beneath me. Where is that first shell going to burst? They don't seem to have spotted us yet. Hardly to be expected, perhaps, when we drop out of the clouds in this fashion!

I hold on to the centre section and stand up on tiptoe to get a view overhead. No, not a shell-burst to be seen! Pleasant though this fact may be, its persistence begins to make me windy.

Hurry up and fire that first shot, *messieurs*!

Infinitely slowly we seem to creep over the trenches. . . .

Whoof! Whoof!

When the long-expected first shell comes, I shudder nervously, but as soon as I see that it has burst several hundred metres behind us, I laugh heartily, and point it out to Engmann.

But the next is better aimed, and the third comes so horribly near us that it removes all traces of mirth from my face. This damned south wind is braking us so heavily that we hardly seem to be moving.

Engmann has put the machine into a gentle turn to get away from the bad patch, but he gains little by his manœuvre. There is a battery of four guns down below, and they are firing shrapnel and shell alternately.

We escape into one of those cloud-bulges that hang down below the main level of the bank, but in a few seconds we fly out again, and once again we are exposed to the gunner's telescope.

I feel very worried. What about turning back? No, I dare not do that because I am ashamed of what Engmann would think of me, even though I know he would hail my decision with relief. But he would never risk retreating unless I gave him express orders to do so, and so we are heroes because each of us is afraid of the other's contempt.

A shrapnel bursts so close to us that the smoke of its explosion passes between our wings a second later.

What about it?

Cold sweat runs down my forehead.

All of a sudden a thin wisp of mist whirls towards us. I cannot call it a cloud; it is just a delicate film that scarcely darkens the sun, and then—hallo! we are bang in the middle of those clouds again—swathes of gauzy stuff below us— growing thicker and thicker—the landscape below us becomes fainter and fainter—now it disappears altogether—and then, all at once we are above the clouds. (See Illustration No. 2.)

I hardly seem able to grasp the fact that we have escaped Archie in this surprising fashion. When at last the truth dawns on me, I cannot restrain my delight.

"Hoi-ho-o!" I shout to Engmann.

When he sees me in the mirror, I describe several circles with the flat of my hand; then I clench my fist and open the fingers out a couple of times, accompanying the gesture with vigorous shakes of my head.

Translated into ordinary speech, this pantomimic effort means: "Well, what do you think of that, old man? We are over the clouds now, and we don't give a damn for Archie."

As Engmann cannot take his hands from the stick or his feet from the rudder-bar, he replies by jogging merrily up and down on his seat over the benzine tank.

Our luck holds good. Ten minutes later the clouds begin to thin out. I can make good observations between the patches, which are nevertheless sufficiently large and numerous to give me cover from any French Archie. The Marne valley is free of clouds; I can see the railway and camp clearly and—what is most important—I have a good view of the Marne bridges west of Châlons. With much satisfaction I photograph them, change the plates and replace the camera. (See Illustration No. 3.)

Then we follow the line of the canal as far as Condé, and, keeping a northwesterly course, head for the Rheims forest. As usual, there are wet cloths of mist over the woods, but here and there I find a gap through which I can make my observations. Photography is, of course, impossible, as the holes in the clouds are too small and too fleeting, and even if I find a large enough opening for my purpose, the clouds cast dark shadows over the landscape. Moreover the open spaces are filmed over with a haze. But what I can see with my eyes will serve my purpose, and I've got the photos of the Marne bridges that H.Q. wants in my pocket—or, more correctly speaking, on my plates.

On we go!

Now we are flying over the tunnel that carries the Epernay-Rheims line beneath the wooded heights. That means we are only ten kilometres away from the front, so that even if Archie hits our engine, we can get home in a glide. And better still, we have the south wind behind us to-day.

"Photography impossible," I thought not so long ago. But now a little incident teaches me how true was Hyde's answer to Cunegaulte: "*Impossible ? Ne me dites jamais cette bête de mot !*"

It happens like this. When I am taking a last look round prior to giving Take the order to glide, a kindly gap in the clouds lets me have a view of the southern entrance to the tunnel. No change there, I see, but a few hundred metres farther south a broad strip of white betrays some new operation. Several narrow curves, projecting from the main

2  ABOVE THE CLOUDS

3  A RAILWAY BRIDGE

*Facing page 46*

line, catch my eye; that means new sidings, I suspect.

Hallo, there's some sort of a move on at Germaine! Rejoicing in my discovery, I signal to Take to cut his engine and give him instructions:

" Fly round in circles until I hit upon a hole through which I can take a photo."

While Take fetches a wide compass, I scan the ground beneath me. Unluckily my view is soon blocked. What a pity! I shall have to possess my soul in patience. I shan't have to wait too long, though, because there's a big gap over yonder that is coming my way. I take the camera from its rack and set the shutter. Then I place the heavy apparatus on the pivotal ring of my machine gun and watch my chance.

The gap in the clouds comes along, but unhappily it passes to the south of me, so that all the view I get is of the uninteresting stretch of ground I have already examined. Meanwhile Engmann has completed a circle; he sounds his throttle and points his hand questioningly in the direction of the front. I shake my head and describe several large circles with my free left arm; that means: " Keep on going round!"

Then I look down again. Wait, there's another gap in the clouds coming along. At last I catch a glimpse of the chalky whiteness that betokens the new operations down below, but this time we are a bit too far south, so that I get only a slanting view. Furthermore the clouds throw heavy shadows across the landscape, which would spoil the photo.

Round we go again. And at last I do the job—or half of it, at least. I get the landscape south of the tunnel free from cloud, but can only catch it obliquely. Still, who knows whether I shall get a chance of a vertical snap to-day, so here goes!
" Click! "

But my ambition remains unsatisfied with this achievement; it wants a vertical picture.

Take Engmann is beginning to get a bit nervous. We have been messing about here for a full quarter of an hour, and though we need not worry about Archie with so much cover from the clouds, there is a French air-squadron at Serniers, only five kilometres farther north. They will have been warned of our presence and are certain to have a shot at nabbing us here—as we seem to be a permanent fixture. We must keep our eyes skinned.

I notice that Engmann is peering all round the horizon, and take advantage of a big hole in the clouds to follow his example. But the air is and remains pleasantly free of hostile aircraft.

Now the tunnel entrance is clear. Click! I've got it. And then something comes into my mind—in " Men," my first book, which was published thirteen months before the War, I wrote a story entitled " The Airman's Death," in which a young officer blows up a French railway tunnel. The tunnel my fantasy pictured was just like the one I have photographed down there. But I am jolly glad that Lieutenant Heydemarck has not been ordered to carry out the fatal mission that he assigned to his fictitious 2nd Lieutenant Heiden.

## THROUGH THE CLOUDS 49

Life is beautiful—or would be, if only I had vertical snaps of those new railway operations.

And now it looks as if I'm going to get them. The landscape is visible—no, there are such heavy shadows from the clouds that it is not worth while wasting a plate.

Round we go again. And then—at last, at last!—I pull it off. My objective lies directly below me, and though there are thick shadows all about it, they will only frame the picture I want to get. A dark patch here and there won't spoil the good general impression.

Click!

Change plates!

Click!

In high glee I release Engmann from further circles by a whack on his helmet. He throttles down a couple of pegs, and makes for the front in a long glide.

. . . . .

When I examined the photos, which turned out quite good in spite of the strong haze, I was puzzled by the four curved railheads they revealed in addition to the ordinary sidings. My supposition that the curves were necessitated by the upward slopes of the ground proved incorrect, for it was subsequently ascertained that these four railheads had nothing to do with the transport facilities. They were in fact, "claws" for a battery of heavy railway artillery—the first of its kind that the French installed in our sector. (See Illustration No. 4 and the sketch at chapter-heading.)

## CHAPTER V

### 1111

AFTER dinner I discussed our orders for the next day with Engmann. " Start at 3 a.m., that means before daybreak. We must be over Epernay at dawn, and we shall have to drop down fairly low if I'm to plant my big bombs fairly and squarely in the railway station."

Take was delighted, as he always is when we have a special job on hand. " How far shall we go down ? " he asked.

I had a bright idea. " We'll drop to 1111 metres," I replied.

Engmann's face was a perfect study. He raised his eyebrows so high that his forehead became a maze of savage wrinkles.

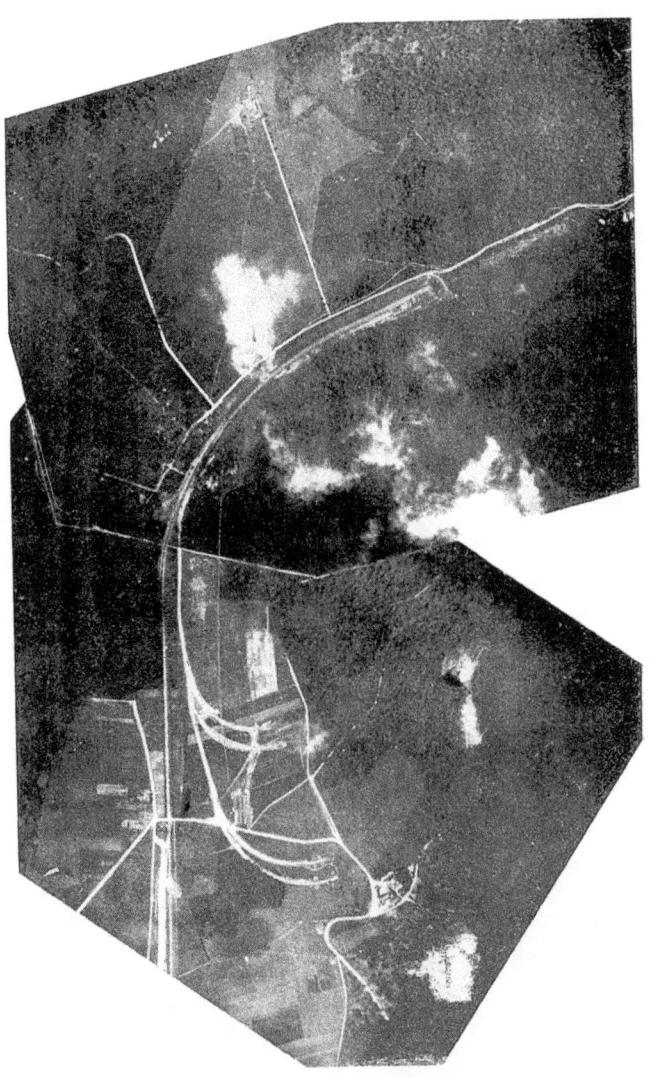

SIDINGS FOR ARMOURED TRAINS

*Facing page* 50

"What? Drop so low when we're so far from home? Supposing we had engine trouble! And why 1111 metres, if I may ask?"

I laughed. "Because it's a number we can easily remember. If you prefer 777, it's all the same to me. Seven's my lucky number."

Engmann screw up his black eyes. "If you want a number we can remember, what about 4711? That's my brand of eau de cologne, and that——"

"Look here, are you trying to pull my leg, young fellow?" I interrupted. "If so, I can kick like a horse."

Engmann shook his head vigorously. "No, no. 1111 will do me."

. . . .

Our start is delayed; the handle of the big bomb is too thick, and we find we cannot fit it in its holder on the rack until it has been filed down. Nevertheless, we get off at 3.10 a.m.

I do a bit of thinking. As we are still some time off daybreak and there is a new moon, we can fly over the front in the dark. So I whack Engmann into the direction of Rheims, but a few minutes later I wonder what sort of a fool I look, for we run into such a thick haze that we seem to be flying in a sea of jelly. Worse still, it swallows up the stars, and even if the minute lights of heaven shed no brightness on our path, we welcome them as fixed points that give us our sense of balance. At present I can get my balance from the flare that still burns in our aerodrome, but as we are flying southwards it lies directly behind us, so that Engmann cannot see it.

We can hardly distinguish anything on the ground beneath us. Only the Aisne Valley, with its damp meadows, stands out in the darkness against its environs, a dark grey mass through which the light grey road runs dimly.

Engmann is getting jumpy; the only point from which he can try to gain a sense of balance is his rev.-counter, the luminous indicator of which emits a faint glow. Then I begin to get unpleasant sensations down my backbone. I must admit that I have lost all sense of direction; my eye can distinguish no landmark in the darkness below me. And if I'm all at sea here, where I know every stick and stone, what is going to happen when we fly over country that is not so familiar? I signal to Engmann to cut his engine.

" Over the Aisne as far as Rethel," I tell him, " and then we'll follow the high road to Rheims."

Engmann nods and puts the machine into a steep right-hand turn, which alters our course to due west. And now I see a faint glow to north-eastward—a pallid, insignificant illumination, but nevertheless a welcome one, because it enables us to identify the horizon. It is the harbinger of the coming dawn that still lingers shyly in the depths.

When we reach Rethel, we have to turn southwest. The change of course puts the morning glow behind our backs. That's a pity—but never mind—now we can grope our way alongside the broad highroad, that runs, straight as a dart, across the landscape. We fly as close to it as possible, as it is a job to pick it out in the haze.

Fifteen minutes later a white gleam reveals the position of the trenches. We pass them without receiving a single shot, and indeed, it would be sheer waste of ammunition for any Archie to pot at us in this soup of a haze.

We fly on, following the road until the houses of Rheims swallow it up. Now we must keep our eyes skinned to spot it when it emerges on the farther side of the town. Ah, there it is, and on we jog, still south-westwards. But unluckily I have no notion that I have picked out the wrong road.

The fact is that the road to Epernay runs due south from Rheims, and meanwhile we are contentedly continuing our old south-western course. In my dazed condition I do not spot my mistake until at last the Marne blinks at us.

As the day gradually dawns, the hitherto monotonous grey of the landscape resolves itself into various distinguishable objects. I can see railways, roads, lanes, fields, villages, and a town.

But surely that can't be Epernay! All the surrounding country is unfamiliar to me. We've never been here before.

We must get our bearings somehow before we cross the river. I switch on my electric torch and compare the map with the landscape, and then I find the solution of the mystery. We are too far west. The little town we see is Dormans—which lies more than twenty kilometres west of Epernay, and so we have blundered into the reconnoitring sphere of the army corps stationed next to our own.

I hastily whack Engmann on his left shoulder; we must follow the Marne upstream.

A glance at the altimeter: 3100 metres. No higher? Well, the weight of that fifty-kilo bomb made climbing difficult.

A bridge over the Marne: that's the one by Boursault Station. Time for us to be dropping, then! "Biff!" Engmann gets a love-tap on his head. He moves his switch slowly back—we glide. A point to be considered: the wind is blowing east here. That means we can head for our objective in our present direction; we do not need to make a detour so as to approach it against the wind. Peering out past the engine, I catch sight of the blurred outlines of Epernay through the bracing-wires, and a happy thought strikes me: hallo! here is something to the good that I did not allow for! As the engine is not kicking up its usual hell of a row, but merely indulging in soft, polite murmurs, I can talk to Engmann and make him understand even if I have to shout a bit.

"Look here, Take, we've got Archie nicely taped. In this lovely mist and this gorgeous twilight they won't be able to see us in any case, and as our engine makes no noise when it's gliding, they won't hear us either."

Engmann manifested his joy with what I call his "polar-bear" expression, that is to say, he wags

his head rhythmically—like a pendulum—left to
right, right to left. Then he begins to play with
the gas-switch so as to prevent the ignition from
becoming fouled with oil and the engine from
drowning in its own benzine. 2200 . . . 2000 . . .
1500 . . . I stand up and take another peep. So
far no one has spotted us. No detonation offends
the morning peace, no shrapnel cloudlet looms out
of the mist. Topping !

Then I curl up in dismay. What—is—up ?

Just now we were wrapped in the faint sheen of
twilight—and now, all of a sudden, it is broad
daylight. Quick as lightning I find the explanation . . . the haze-bank only extends to 1,300
metres. We have gone through it and are now
flying underneath. Hence this amazing brightness !

The shock of seeing himself shown up in his true
light does not fail to produce its effect on Engmann.
I see him bend over to push the switch forward.
I grab at his arm, and obediently he withdraws
his hand, but his eyes squint mistrustfully at the
town that looms so near.

Inexorably I shake my head.

" IIII ! And don't open out until I've dropped
my bomb ! "

I can sympathize with his discomfort. It is
most uncanny to drop so low when we are so far
from home. It puts all sorts of silly notions into
one's head, because a good height is our strongest
asset. When our bomb has exploded, single-
seaters and Archie will be after our blood, and

to-day they will be less welcome than ever. If they hit our engine at this low height, we have no chance of getting back.

All the same we are going down to 1111 metres because we said we would!

I look ahead again. All the houses rising up out of the white streets look wonderfully real. I can see the outlines of the long, wide bridge. The waters of the Marne are foaming up over the parapet, and I imagine I can hear their murmur through the wind whistling in the bracing-wires.

Slowly the station rolls towards us. There are many rows of trucks on the lines—an engine stands ready, with steam up—a whole village of sheds—it's a good target!

I glance at the altimeter. The slim indicator is nearly down to 1100, and the pencil has scribbled a similar record on the barogram.[1] We have kept our promise and are going to drop that bomb

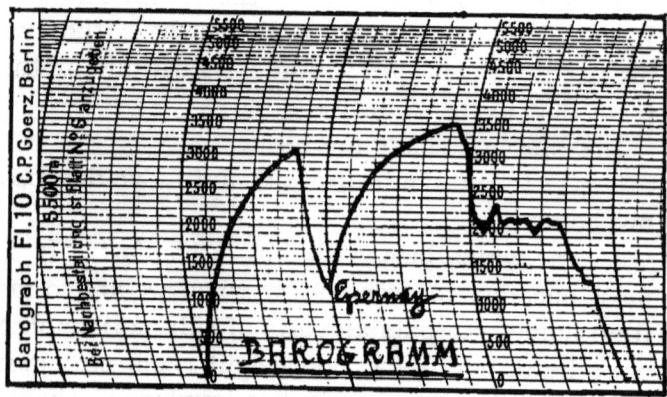

[1] The air-pressure curves on the paper also record the varying heights

from a height that we can assume to be 1111 metres. I sight my objective. Shall I let go? No, better wait a few seconds—no—not yet—now then—down she goes! Bump!

Through the spyhole in the floor my eye follows the progress of the falling monster. Then I have to laugh—no need to instruct my good Take to open out his engine. In every nerve of his body he felt the jerk that the bomb made when it left the machine, and the very next second he pushed the switch forward. Holding my breath, I listen to the ever-swelling drone of the engine. It is clear and even; despite the long glide the ignition has not been fouled. I draw a deep breath of relief.

Engmann flies a straight course, and so I contrive to keep the bomb in sight. I see it grow smaller and smaller.

But——

My heart is oppressed with dreadful misgivings; that bomb is not going to fall on the station, but in the middle of the town! When we were flying at 3100 the wind was blowing from the east, but down here it is a north wind. The proof is that we are drifting southward. In fact the wind must have got up a lot, because it is driving us very considerably out of our course. The station disappears completely from my spyhole, and now I can only see the house beneath us, down upon which my heavy bomb is falling!

I have still a faint hope. I can see a big square; perhaps the bomb will fall in the middle of it. All the window-panes of the neighbouring houses will be shivered to smithereens, but that will be the sole damage. With all my heart I hope that this may happen.

But my hopes are vain. Now the bomb has reached the ground. Horrible! the cloud caused by its explosion does not arise from the square, but from a big house at the corner.

A fresh hope dawns in me. Perhaps it is not a dwelling-house but a public building. I cannot bear to think that I may have killed women . . . perhaps even children!

But no pangs of remorse can undo my error. I have only one idea—to get away from this place where I have wrought such evil!

Never have we flown so slowly, it seems to me. At such a low altitude the landscape generally races away from us, but to-day it appears to creep at a snail's pace.

And to know that howe'er I clench my teeth and exert my will, I cannot spur our aeroplane on to a speedier pace—that is the worst of all! I have no spurs on my boots, no whip in my hand, like you, oh happy horseman! I can only crouch idle and inactive in my seat. If only I could prick my steed's flanks and crack the whip round his legs until he shot forward like an arrow from the bow —onward, ever onward—but such relief is denied the flying man.

The town is still in sight. Hesitatingly I look back to note the effect produced by my wretched bomb. A thick cloud of smoke and dust rises from the stricken building, and it is to me as if the curses hurled up to us by a thousand fists weigh like lead upon our wings and ban us to the site of our crime. The hatred that fills the souls of those folk below gives them power over us as long as we are still within their sight and earshot.

Laboriously we fight against the north wind that opposes us so obstinately. At last we have reached the Marne and risen to 1300 metres, so that the haze envelops us once more in its protective mantle. It puts no invisible cap on our heads to hide us completely from the denizens of earth, but Archie and aviators will have harder work to find us.

What's up with those Archie? We haven't had a single shot. There is only one explanation. The unusual course we took in approaching the town has combined with the haze, the twilight and our glide to obviate all signs of our attack. The gunners knew nothing about us until roused by the explosion of our bomb. I can still see Epernay behind us. I do not want to look back again—and yet I must.

I am usually so delighted with a direct hit! But this time I curse the bomb. If only it had failed to explode, or if at least it had only been a small one—but that monster weighed a hundredweight!

Luckily I am unable to brood over these gloomy thoughts because I have to make observations. From Ay station a white stream of smoke appears; through my glasses I count forty-seven trucks—open and covered. Some have white hoods over them.

I make the entry on my map, and then search the high road with my glasses. No, nothing more to be seen.

A small surprise. Far behind me, to westward of the town, a ray of light springs up from the ground and flickers in the air like a will-o'-the-wisp. I have to laugh. "If you've only just woken up to our presence, young fellow," I think, "by the time you've got our direction fixed, your mirror will gleam as faintly as a cyclist's oil lamp."

Then I shudder: Engmann has cut his engine. I turn round quickly. What's up? From his open mouth his teeth grin at me in his mirror. Then he points upward and opens out his fingers from a clenched fist. Archie!

I follow the direction of his outstretched arm. High above us in the sea of mist shells and shrapnels are bursting in rapid succession. They look like gleams from a pocket-torch or a firework of sorts. Now we must try to lull those gunners into the pleasing belief that they have found the range.

"Half-right," I order Engmann with a whack on the right shoulder. And, lo and behold, the shell-cloudlets follow our course, but always a thousand metres too high. We grin gleefully at one another in the mirror.

This comedy, however, could easily turn into a tragedy. The explosion of our bomb will be known at the neighbouring aerodromes by now, and in all likelihood the first *avions de chasse* have started to look for us. No doubt it will be hard for them to find us in the dim light of the early morning, but now that our homeward path is plainly indicated by rows of cotton-wool cloudlets, we must be prepared for unpleasant surprises, the more so as this vile headwind reduces our pace to a crawl.

At St. Etienne red flares are burning, at Suippes a beacon. It is most probable that from both these aerodromes avengers have gone aloft in search of us.

Via St. Hilaire junction we push our way to Somme-Bionne, where I must make my observations of the camp. Every moment I expect to see those Nieuports heading for us, but none make their appearance.

Meanwhile, although we have to fight against the wind, the release of the bomb has reduced our weight, and so we have managed to climb to 3500 metres.

The fire of Archie at Bussy-le-Château is so miserable that I dismiss it from my mind with a pitying laugh. The kindly haze covers us splendidly; the gunners below have only the drone of our engine to guide them, and as the north-east wind is giving us a strong drift, their shots go amazingly wide of the mark. I rejoice wholeheartedly at the fleecy cloudlets that make their appearances almost a whole kilometre to our left.

"Tirrp! Tirrp! Tirrp!"

Engmann sounds his throttle three times; I stand up to follow the direction of his outstretched arm, and catch sight of a Nieuport flying on our level and only 400 metres away. So in spite of their woeful marksmanship the Archie have done good work by pointing out our path to their airmen. It is true that one swallow does not make a summer, but there are certain to be a few more close at hand.

Meanwhile the French pilot has circled round and risen above us. Now he hovers directly behind us; I swing my machine gun round and joyfully await his attack.

"I may have to wait some time," I think, chuckling. "He'll certainly not dare to go for us single-handed; he'll hang about till a couple of his pals come up."

I am right. He hovers over us like a hawk above a poultry run, but as he knows that this little chick can look after itself, he takes care not to come to grips with it.

But though the young fellow fails to impress me, his presence here is disagreeable. How am I to make calm and accurate observations with a sword of Damocles hanging over my head?

I begin to get fed up with the business. But by old experience I know that shooting is often infectious. Having warned Engmann, I therefore send a series of shots in the direction of our shadower.

And, sure enough, he catches the infection! After accomplishing the usual fearsome turn, he dives on us, rattling away with his machine gun. Take starts zigzagging, while I watch for the Frenchman to run into my fire. I feel quite calm and a tiny bit superior—only one enemy to deal with! What harm can he do us?

The haze is so thick that I completely lose sight of the Frenchman when Engmann makes a somewhat wider turn. I cannot blame my good Take; he has to depend entirely on me in such affairs, for he cannot know what is happening behind his back. The mirror is his only means of watching my fights, and to-day he can hardly see our opponent in the dense haze. But he hears a machine gun hammering away at us from somewhere in the grey void, and in spite of its monotony this melody is liable to get on one's nerves. When the Frenchman comes into my sights after our turn is over, I blaze away again. A comic idea comes into my head as I shoot: what would happen if two of our bullets met in the air? Would they burst? I hardly think so; probably they would knock each other backward.

Through the haze the Nieuport looks just like two strokes with a blob in the middle. It would seem as if I have hit its engine, as it is puffing away like an old steam-tug on the Havel river.

Not a bad pilot either to attack me so ferociously without a pal to help him!

But now the stream of bluish-white smoke thickens. *M. l'aviateur* goes over on to his right wing and makes off.

After him! We'll finish him off! I quickly signal to Take, who makes a lightning turn—there's the Frenchman again. The thick cloud of gleaming smoke he leaves behind him resembles nothing so much as the tail of a running animal, on to which we hang like a fawn behind its doe. (See sketch at chapter heading.) But as the Nieuport is the speedier machine, our vision of it soon dwindles. I can't help laughing at old Take, because he won't give up the chase; that is always the way—a fleeing enemy excites one's combative ardour to white heat.

I therefore have to damp Take's pugnacity with a whack on the shoulder. Unwillingly he obeys me and puts our machine into a right-hand turn.

I glance at the altimeter. Our hunting fever has brought us down to 2000 metres. We must not go any lower as long as we are on the French side of the front, for after dropping our bomb into the Epernay wasps'-nest we are bound to find swarms of stinging-insects about.

So home once more!

The few kilometres between us and the front are fairly plastered with shells and shrapnels. But the blessed haze wraps us round with its covering mantle, and the shots do not even come near enough to warm the air for us.

We pass our own trenches without having received a single hit.

## CHAPTER VI

### SEEING IT THROUGH

WITH two twenty-kilo bombs on board and an atmosphere so rarefied that it hardly seems to hold our wings we find it difficult to gain height to-day. When we have only reached 2,200 after a whole hour's climbing, I see that any further spirals will be sheer waste of time and whack Engmann to the front via Rheims.

We have a bit of luck and find a cloudbank over the trenches. It is only somewhere between two and three kilometres wide and not particularly thick; when we are flying above it we can see the positions below, as through a thick veil.

We must help Nature to thicken the covering

she has given us. As the sun's position is half-left, I let Engmann manœuvre our machine onto the extreme right edge of the clouds; thus I increase the thickness between us and the battery on our left, which is our most dangerous foe because its gunners have the sun at their backs. This means, of course, that we have less cover against the battery to our right, but there the gunners are handicapped by having the sun in their eyes when they shoot. My theory works out in practice, for we cross the lines untouched.

Once behind the front we find things easier, for over the Rheims woods we run into further patches of cloud which afford us good cover to snuggle up into.

.   .   .   .

We have photographed Châlons and the St. Etienne aerodrome. We have only to unload our two twenty-kilo bombs on to Mourmelon camp; then our job is done.

After whacking Engmann into a north-west course I make a systematic search of the air because I don't want to be surprised by any enemy when approaching my objective.

My precaution seems unnecessary. Everything is just as it should be—no, not quite, though, for there's something flying our way from over there on the left. I put my glasses to my eyes; it turns out to be a double-decker with a lattice tail! French machine, therefore, and apparently a Caudron.

No more chances of a direct approach to our

objective. If my head disappears into the cockpit for even a couple of seconds, that fellow will attack me. Better see if we can shake him off! I bend over to Engmann and point him out the double-engined machine.

"Go for him!"

But just as Take is about to put the bus into a turn to attack this opponent, he suddenly checks himself and waves his hand to my right. I follow its direction and see a Nieuport approaching. I have to laugh as I swing my machine gun round to repel its assault; no wonder I nearly missed the little chap! Formerly all French single-seaters were painted light blue and bore two red, white and blue cockades on the upper wings, but now they have changed their colour to a brown-green so that only their movements show them up against the landscape beneath.

Under the circumstances we must let the Caudron go in peace; I therefore signal Engmann to fly straight ahead again. The next moment the little Nieuport shoots by us on our level and turns to attack our tail. As we shoot ahead, it looks as though the wind catches him in his curve and pushes him back. Nice for us; we gain a good start which I use to make further observations and photograph another camp.

We must take care the Caudron doesn't spring a surprise on us from below while I'm sparring with the Nieuport. I scan the sky carefully, but can see no sign of the big fellow. Has he lost sight of us so soon? Most unlikely when the sky's as clear as it is to-day. Hm, there's some dirty work going on; we'll have to look out for ourselves.

The next moment it flashes across my brain: "Damn it all, you've still got your bombs on board! You're surely not going to fight with them in the machine!" I look down quickly—any decent mark in the neighbourhood? No! There are a couple of small camps, of course, on our way, but to bring the machine round against the wind, fly carefully over the objective and take good aim with that Nieuport hanging on our tail—it would be sheer suicide. And as for trying to drop them while flying in our present direction, we'd be bound to make a mess of it with this crosswind drifting us off the mark.

No, we must find a big target where our aiming doesn't need to be dead accurate. Perhaps we can push on to Mourmelon in spite of our shadower—it's not so far away. We'll see if the Nieuport lets us do it.

One thing's certain: I'm not going to chuck my eggs into some empty field on the chance that the Frenchman might put a shot into their detonators—no, it simply can't be done. I'm too fond of my bombs for that; I can't screw myself to throw away forty kilos of steel and explosives. I'd rather take the risk.

But first of all I'll try the old trick that has diddled many a Frenchman. And, lo and behold, I have hardly got Take to head the machine for the front when the Nieuport turns away and bears off to the south. Probably the pilot thinks:

"My job is done; I've scared the *avion boche* away. It would be ungentlemanly of me to bother about him any more."

I give a signal to Engmann, who grins knowingly in his mirror and turns back into our old course.

Topping to think that I've put it across the Nieuport with my little trick and can now fly unmolested to our objective. Naturally I take another look round, and just as well I do—why, there's the fellow again!

I can't help laughing. He's just like old Cæsar, the black sheepdog I had before the War! When he followed me out riding and I sent him home, he always trotted off obediently, but if I looked round at the next corner, I could be certain to see him pop up again somewhere in the rear.

This French César is apparently just as affectionate as my German Cæsar; rather more so perhaps in the matter of hanging on to me. I bend over to Engmann and get him to cut his engine so that I can give him directions how to approach our objective. Suddenly we both quiver at the sound of distant machine gun fire; is there going to be a fight sprung on us while we are twisting our way to our goal, or are we being peppered by someone down below? When I look round, I see something that makes me give a respectful gasp. But I recover quickly and pass the news on to Engmann—the Nieuport has opened hostilities and is potting at us from a record distance of 1,000 metres!

Engmann promptly goes into a turn in order to have a look at this strange phenomenon. When he has personally convinced himself of the truth of my incredible news, we both laugh till the tears run down our cheeks. In airfights there is only one slogan, and that is : " Go for your man ! "

Naturally the French have many dashing pilots who know this slogan, and act upon it. I need only mention Navarre, the ace, and de Terline was another who went all out. In his fight with Freytag he dived so furiously that he rammed my comrade.

But this chicken-hearted fellow must have no feeling of shame left in him if he can open fire at a distance that is almost astronomical in its magnitude as far as airfights are concerned. From across the void I hear his old coffee-machine continuing to grind out its faint song.

" Dagg dagg dagg dagg dagg dagg! "

When out of pure devilment I send a series of shots in his direction, he shows his respect of me by going into a nervous turn. Some of his comrades may not be exactly heroes when called upon to engage in single combat, but none of them have given me quite such an easy job as this bright specimen. He is probably a raw beginner ; if so, we can regard him as a negligible quantity and go ahead just as if he wasn't there.

I look ahead : the barracks are plainly visible. I signal Engmann to steer a direct course for them. But now the Nieuport pilot seems to have shot some spunk into himself and forges ahead as though he meant business. He is within 400 metres of us.

To test his intelligence I signal Take to turn off in the direction of the front again. This time our adversary sees through the trick and hangs on to us. Bravo, my little lad! You've guessed we're up to some mischief round Mourmelon way, and you're out to stop it if you can.

Whoof!

Involuntarily I flinch as the first shell bursts close to us on the left. The brute was most disagreeably near! That means that we are within range of the camp Archie, and without waiting for orders Engmann goes into a turn.

Hi-ee-ee-ee!

Where's the next going to burst?

And whoof! there it is! Elevation perfect, but 200 metres to our rear, and I burst out laughing. It's bang in front of the Nieuport's nose! Hope he'll like the smell of it!

But the Nieuport pilot has had enough; he pulls his machine round and makes off southward. We utilize the opportunity and head for Mourmelon again. All around us is a raging turmoil of shells and shrapnels. Can I pull it off?

Where's the Nieuport? Not a sign of him anywhere!

While Engmann zizgags his way to our objective, I take a look round. Nothing to be seen! Most suspicious. At last, when I hang out and look down, I spy him; the cunning little blighter has got in under our tail and means to attack us again. As his bus carries a pivotable machine gun on the upper wing he can fire either forward or vertically upward. (See sketch at chapter heading.) Such attacks from the dead angle where I cannot reach my assailant are as painful to me as a tickling on the soles of the feet is to the average man.

Under the circumstances we must clear off and give up the idea of bombing Mourmelon. The little Nieuport whom we despised has turned out a mighty adversary, worthy of our respect. He goes into a turn, and then comes at us again.

Whoof!

Another shell. And this time it bursts so near the Nieuport that he turns away in high dudgeon and says good-bye to us. When I have whacked Engmann a bit to the right and shown him the departing Frenchman, he wriggles about on his seat with delight. The relief braces our nerves. Now everything in the garden is lovely—except the business with the bomb.

Where are we going to drop it? Not in this part of the world, for here we are within the range of our own heavy artillery, and why should we butt in on to their job? As for taking my eggs home again—simply out of the question. I bend over and put my mouth to Engmann's ear.

"Bombs!"

When Take has cut his engine and stares round at me in amazement, I explain the business to him.

"I'm not going to chuck them away in a field just because of that silly Nieuport. As soon as we've seen the last of him, we'll get off to Suippes and put them down on the station."

But as soon as Engmann has put the machine into a steep right-hand turn to make for the station we hear the distant sound of a machine gun. I turn round irritably—HE is there again. Now I am thoroughly fed up. He's like a louse in one's skin that one can't get rid of—a most painful business. And as the station Archie have brought themselves to my notice with a couple of shells, I whack Engmann into the direction of the front. I can gladly stick a bit of machine gun fire for my bombs' sake, but this constant peppering is bound to end up with some silly chance shot hitting their detonators. I'm not out to gamble everything on a single throw, and I've no desire to take the risk.

While Engmann is making for Aubérive, I open fire on the blighter again. In my wrath I waste a whole drum of ammunition, but it seems to put the fear of the Lord into him.

When he turns off southward, I decide to turn back and unload my bombs on Suippes. But the Nieuport won't trust us out of his sight; he has gone into another turn and is looking for a chance to get at us.

Once more his machine gun rattles away at us. I utilize an interval in his fire to photograph him, for, enraged as I am, I must say that I am impressed with his speedy development from a platonic friend of the most distant sort to a really affectionate wooer. (See Illustration No. 5.)

But this game has got to stop. As it always rouses me when I find anyone who can do my job better than I can, I feel I want to finish off my opponent. I want to, but I simply can't, unfortunately, for as he sticks fast under my tail, I have to fire almost vertically downwards, with the result that my gun goes into one jam after another. To turn about and attack him is equally useless, because a single-seater is faster and more agile than my machine, and moreover, its pilot always makes off as soon as he hears the sound of my gun. And so, despite the blow to my pride, I have to admit that for all his cautious tactics that Frenchman has not merely proved a hindrance; he has actually prevented me from carrying out my job.

I swallow the bitter fact and spit it out again. I'm going to see the business through somehow!

Having taken this decision I can pull myself together again. And now my soul is at peace once more.

As we are no longer under fire from any set of Archie, I have leisure to study the lie of the land. South of St. Souplet the German trenches are wrapped in a greenish-yellow haze: gas! Poison gas! What a blessing there's nothing of that sort (not yet, at least) up in the air!

"Go on as far as Pont-Faverger so that we can get rid of the Nieuport. Then back across the front to Mourmelon, which was, is, and still shall be our objective."

Engmann goes into a wide turn and crosses the trenches at Prosnes. Archie has heard the drone of our engine and put up a thick barrage. Never mind, we're going through it!

5   A NIEUPORT CLIMBING TO ATTACK US

*Facing page* 74

As we zigzag our way to our goal, I comb out the air around me. No sign of the Nieuport or any other aircraft.

With a sigh of satisfaction I duck into the cockpit and release the safety catch on the bomb-rack. Bomb No. 1—Knack! Bomb No. 2—Knick!

Well?

With an idiotic grin on my face I stare at No. 2's empty place. Bomb No. 2 has certainly left—taken French leave, I might say—but my smile freezes on my mouth when I grasp the situation. What if I've unloaded that bomb onto German territory! Refusing to follow this uncomfortable idea to its logical end, I prefer to look down and see whether my chance effort has really sent the twenty-kilo fellow.

I search the ground beneath me and can scarcely believe my eyes. We are flying over the little woodland camp at Pyramide, and my bomb has dropped bang in the middle of it! (See Illustration No. 6.)

Out with the camera, and we'll have a snap of it! When I have changed the plates and put the camera back, I have a look at our original objective. Quickly the town of barracks rolls up; it is so large that with the best will in the world I can't miss it.

I get it in my sights. Ah, that's the right angle. I pull the lever sharply; down goes the other twenty-kilo fellow!

Whoof! Whoof! to right and left of us. Doesn't matter now, for I'm through with the job.

I press Engmann's left shoulder, then hang over to peer in the mirror in which his eyes are seeking my own. " Home, Take ! "

While we go into a turn I take up my camera and withdraw the cap. I must have a snap of the camp.

But my humbled pride causes me swiftly to renounce all thoughts of what would have been a most interesting photo, for I see that my bomb has gone absolutely wide of the mark. There is the big camp which I thought it was impossible to miss, and there is my bomb on an open field, where there's not a soul about !

I've actually done the impossible and missed that huge target. But why ? how ? wherefore ? Have I miscalculated ? Did a sudden breeze spring up and develop into a gale ? That lucky shot in the Pyramide camp is but a faint consolation for my disappointment.

And why on earth did Bomb No. 2 take leave of us in such sudden fashion ?

Full of curiosity, I investigate the apparatus. Ah, so that is the solution of the mystery : the wire cable is broken, though whether through a flaw in the material or a chance shot in my fight with the Nieuport, I cannot say. At all events, things have turned out as they so often do in life : when I tried to do something, I made a mess of it, and when it did itself, it pulled off a success. With a fatalistic shrug of the shoulders I resign myself to the inevitable.

While Engmann is heading for the front with an

Photograph of a Direct Hit on the "Pyramide" Camp

open throttle and thus bringing a row of shrapnel cloudlets in our wake, I look back once more. Yes, there's a speck in the air! I have a presentiment, which is justified when I put my glasses to my eyes and discover an aeroplane silhouetted against the blue sky. Our faithful Nieuport! As I have got rid of the bombs and so done my job I feel really quite pleased to see him again!

I signal Engmann into a short right-hand turn and show him our aerial policeman. We are genuinely pleased to give him full marks for his sleuthing abilities because we are pleased with ourselves.

*Quand même,* in spite of everything—we have seen the business through!

# CHAPTER VII

### ENGINE TROUBLE

UNLESS I gave him special instructions, my batsman's standing orders were as follows: "Wake me at 6 a.m., using your own discretion."

"Using your own discretion" meant "If it's flying weather." And so, using his discretion, Hugo let me slumber on in peace one morning, because the sky was covered with thick clouds.

But about seven I was roused by Engmann, who could blow in at any time unannounced. After bidding me good morning, he began to fidget about from one foot to another.

"Well, Take, what's vexing your soul? Out with it!"

At last he got it off his chest. "I've still got

# ENGINE TROUBLE

to do two outside landings to qualify for my pilot's badge. And as we can't fly over the front to-day on account of the clouds, I wanted to ask whether we might perhaps——"

" All right," I interrupted him. " This afternoon at three."

. . . . .

Unfortunately there is a short delay before our start because the engine is found to be quite 200 revs. down. When our mechanics have changed the sparking plugs, they tune it up to 1320. So off we go!

Squadron 22 is our first landing. But shortly before we reach Lessingcourt the trouble begins again.

Blubbblubb!—blub! blubblub!—blubblubb-blub!

Our hearts begin knocking too. But we just manage to reach the aerodrome.

After an overhaul we start off for A. 212.[1] In a long glide our engine gives signs of further distress, but somehow we contrive to stagger along to Bémont-Ferme.

With the assistance of the shop-superintendent we examine the patient's weak heart thoroughly for the usual symptoms. We inspect the carburetter, magneto, and distributor, but can find nothing wrong. When Take lets the engine run I put my foot in the step and pull myself up until I can see the rev.-counter. Its indicator is vibrating between 1240 and 1260.

[1] Artillery flyers, Squadron No. 212.

We can therefore risk starting off to No. 10 squadron. But it is written that man shall not tempt the gods—and this time we are really in trouble.

Blubblubblubblubb—blubb!

As it is obviously impossible to reach Merland Ferme, we look out for an emergency landing-place. Near St. Clément there are some stretches of fallow ground, on which we can put the machine down without much trouble.

Blubb——?

The engine has gone dead. I hope to goodness we can reach some level ground, for if Take should happen to crash his machine when engaged on completing his final test, he would have to wait a long time for that pilot's badge.

Down we glide. In the clearing just before the pine woods there is a splendid field, but in his efforts to reach it Engmann puts the stick so far over that we go down in a nosedive. Result: we have to even out—the beautiful field rolls away from under us—and the next moment we are over the long stretch of wood. A good thing the trees are fairly low; even so, Engmann almost scrapes their topmost branches. Anxious question: have we sufficient power in our machine to clear the wood? Smiling sadly as I resign myself to my fate, I think of those little rhymes that we recited so often in our pupil days.

> If you crash in a wood, it is most absurd
>   To think of resuming your flight.
> So just sit on a tree like a little bird,
>   And sing to your heart's delight.

Engmann tries every trick he knows to prolong the glide—and he succeeds! We clear the wood and land in a field on its farther side. As there is scarcely any way left on the machine, we taxi only a few metres.

What next? We must have a shot at reaching No. 10's aerodrome, where we shall find tools and mechanics to patch up our engine sufficiently for it to take us back to Attigny.

First we give all the cylinders a dose of petrol; then we swing the propeller three times so as to make sure that the piston is doing its duty. Then we take a brief rest to let the engine cool.

Engmann sets the engine running again, and as it seems to be making its proper number of revs. once more, we take off and make a good landing at Merland-Ferme.

After giving the engine a thorough overhauling, we start homeward in the twilight. We climb to a decent height; then the engine begins to blubber again. With our hearts in our mouths for the next quarter of an hour we just manage to make our own aerodrome.

When we have restored some vigour to our nervous knees, I take hold of Engmann's ear.

"Aren't you ashamed of yourself, Take, to invite me to your trials for that silly old pilot's badge and then bring me out in a machine in that miserable condition?"

He shrugged his shoulders. "Yes, Herr Lieutenant, the engine . . ."

"I know a certain little poem," I interrupted him.

> When you've written off a bus,
> About the engine make a fuss.
> Say it had no revs. at all,
> Say the pressure was too small.
> If you think such lies too lame,
> Stick or prop can bear the blame.
> Then curse about the piston rings;
> The inlet valves had rotten springs.
> Everything in fact was frail,
> Except the liar who pitched the tale.

Engmann laughed. "Alas, too true," he admitted.

. . . . .

A few weeks later (after Captain Mohr had pinned the pilot's badge on to the chest of the modestly blushing Take) we took the afternoon patrol one day.

Some thick stuff was blowing over from southward, so that I was afraid Châlons would be covered before we could get there. But the Marne hindered the further progress of the clouds, which piled themselves up into huge masses on the farther side. It was a phenomenon we had often observed; the moisture-laden air that rises from the valleys of large rivers catches the clouds as they sail by and holds them.

We therefore flew down the Marne as far as Epernay. As there were a few gaps in the masses on the southern bank, I got a glimpse through the veil here and there.

## ENGINE TROUBLE

South of Matougues I made an important discovery; five new hangars were in process of building. There was nothing remarkable about the number of them, but their size astonished me; I had never seen such large erections on our front before. As I subsequently estimated from the photograph I took, each of these hangars must have measured 52 by 40 metres, making therefore an area of more than 2000 square metres. There could be no possible doubt about the use to which they were going to be put: they were destined to house a bombing squadron.

Unfortunately I was unable to get the details of these new buildings on to my plate because I could only get a slanting photo through a gap in the clouds. Before we could fly overhead for a vertical exposure, they were covered up again.

I decided to refrain from reporting these new hangars until I could get a better photo of them. " Honey is sweet " is an airman's saying, and so I wanted to keep all the kudos for myself.

*Au revoir*, dear hangars, *au revoir*!

When we landed and I informed Engmann of my intention, he winked. " I'll cross my thumbs," he said, " so as to stop anyone else finding them till we can get busy again. And, what's more, I'll pray for bad weather until our next patrol."

. . . .

His egoistic wish was granted. After a succession of idle days, dripping with rain and dark with clouds, the first flight was assigned to us.

There was a slight drizzle during the morning, but in the afternoon it cleared up.

Standing at Engmann's side beside our machine, I found myself in two minds about the business. Should we take off at once, so as to make sure of a photo, or would it be better to wait a while and do the job when the sun was lower? If I could get a picture with long shadows, our staff would be able to deduce certain facts about the nature of the buildings. But as I concluded that a bird in hand is worth two in the bush, we took off at once.

. . . . .

We have zoomed up behind the front.

I bend down to attend to my camera, but promptly raise my head again. Engmann has sounded his throttle.

"What's up?"

He points to the rev.-counter.

The indicator wobbles about uneasily. It ought to stand at 1350, and now it drops slowly to 1200 —1100—1000. After thinking matters over there, it comes to a sudden decision and jumps right up to 1500. It only stays a couple of seconds there; then it slides back to 800.

Shrugging his shoulders, Engmann seeks to read my face in the mirror. We hold our breath and listen to the engine's iron chant. It is a clear note, full of vigour—everything O.K.! The St. Vitus dance executed by the indicator can only imply that the rev.-counter itself is out of order. Probably the connecting-rod has stuck.

Yes, that's the trouble! Suddenly the indicator

makes another big drop to zero, although the engine carries on as usual.

Then the rev.-counter goes completely dotty. The indicator stands still, but the dial begins to dance about. Engmann taps his forehead and laughs.

I glance at the altimeter: 2400 metres. A couple of minutes ago it registered only 2100. That proves that the rev.-counter has struck work.

We fly on towards the front; the business is not worth bothering about. Piloted by a raw hand, I should have thought twice about flying over the enemy's lines without a rev.-counter. But Take works by his own flying-sense rather than by the rev.-counter. If a gust catches our machine, he knows at once whether she will stand on her nose or rear up on her tail.

All the same, it is a nasty business flying without the rev.-counter, which is and always will be our best friend up aloft. It is indispensable in clouds and fogs, when the eye can find no fixed point from which to gain a sense of balance.

But, above all, it is the faithful servant that records the engine's pulse-beats, upon the normality of which our lives—or at least our liberty—depend. Luckily it is a most exceptional proceeding for the engine to go dead suddenly and without warning; generally it proclaims its sickness by a gradual slacking off. We are consequently very loth to dispense with the rev.-counter's good advice.

But if we land to get a new one, we shall waste

a lot of time, and most likely the clouds will cover those new hangars again. No, it can't be done.

Besides, our engine has never yet left us in the lurch during a flight over enemy territory. Why then should it take it into its head to follow the rev.-counter's bad example to-day? But as, like all airmen, I am superstitious, I take the precaution of murmuring the usual exorcism:

" Toi! toi! toi!"

. . . . .

We are lucky to-day; scarcely one shell follows us when we cross the enemy's lines on a bridge of clouds. Despite the haze it is easy to observe, and there are no hostile machines in the air. But when I am taking a look round, my eye falls by chance on the altimeter.

3400 metres!

3400?

Why? We were at 3500 a moment ago!

But my misgivings are quickly allayed. In all probability we have run into a patch of thin air, and in such cases one often drops 100 or even 200 metres without warning. Oh, carry on!

Peering out beyond the engine I catch sight of the new big hangars. Funny that no one else has spotted them as yet!

With some reluctance I glance at the altimeter again. Now it stands at only 3300. The whole business is so uncanny that I should like nothing better than to whack Engmann back to our own lines. But despite the danger signal I cannot bring myself to do it; I must get those hangars

## ENGINE TROUBLE

on my plate first. Question: can we reach them before Engmann smells a rat?

In case the worst comes to the worst, I'll make sure of a slanting photo, anyhow. So I get my camera out, focus the hangars between our wings and press the release. Good work! Now let's hope I can manage a vertical snap as well.

Just before we reach our objective, I put my glasses to my eyes. Four hangars are finished, the fifth is nearing completion. I can see the scaffolding about it quite plainly. As we fly over it, I take up my camera once more and focus for a vertical photo. Click! the job is done. Now to change the plate-holders quickly and expose a second plate so that the photography department can make use of it in the stereoscopic apparatus. (See Illustration No. 7.)

Just as I cap my lens I hear something that sets my knees knocking.

Blubb! Blubbubbubbb! Blubbub!

Our engine is in trouble again!

At once Engmann goes into a left-hand turn. He has only one idea in his head: back to the front by the shortest way!

A series of visions flits through my brain—landing in enemy territory—set machine on fire—oh, Lord, I haven't got an officer's cap with me to-day—only the fur cap I'm wearing! Instinctively my fingers feel for the edges of my tunic under the leather jacket—where my mother sewed in a couple of gold coins—a present from my father—to help me escape if ever I am taken prisoner.

But the next moment I pull myself together. Silly ass! You haven't lost the game yet!

Surely Fate is on our side, for we contrive to slink past Châlons unnoticed! If Archie there had spotted us, we should have been forced into turns to dodge their shells and shrapnels, thus losing precious height. And if they had heard our engine blubbering they'd have given us hell with their quick fire. But going north via Matougues we shall fly over territory where there is no Archie. One bit of luck, at least!

I cast a benevolent eye over the town, and, yielding to the irony of the situation, take a slanting snap of the crowded station—a bit of gallows' humour on my part! Then I glance at the altimeter again; it has now fallen from its original 3500 to 3100. And we are still thirty kilometres behind the front.

What's wrong? What's wrong with that engine? Did a shrapnel bullet or a shell splinter hit it when we crossed the front on the outward journey? or a valve, perhaps? Or the water-pump? Or maybe there's a hole in the crankcase?

Our eyes search the engine's surface, but the rapid ups and downs of the valve motion render it impossible to discern the cause of the trouble. Yet unmistakably enough the irregular beats hammer the ghastly truth home to our ears:

Blubb! Blubb! Blubbubb!

That means the end of our alarums and excursions. For the rest of the war we can kick our heels in some prison camp in the south of France.

7     THE FRENCH AERODROME AT MATOUGES

*Facing page* 88

# ENGINE TROUBLE

No more flying for us—for months—perhaps even for years—oh hell!

I choke down these gloomy forebodings. We are still free—still at large—we have still the power of action. All of a sudden I bend over to Engmann and shout instructions in his ear :

" Nose dive—maybe a valve's gone wrong ! "

If that is the cause of the trouble, our swift downward rush may cure the trouble. Take nods and pushes the stick over so energetically that I bump my head against a strut.

He evens out ; then he repeats the procedure.

" Hi—ee—ee—ee ! " whistles the air in our wires.

We hold our breath to listen to the engine's note.

" Blubb ! Blubbubbb ! "

As this drastic treatment has not cured the patient, we must look for other symptoms of his disease.

My knees tremble as I look at the altimeter. 2600. We are dropping lower and lower all the time, and now it seems as if a block of three cylinders has gone on strike. But their pistons are kept moving by the others, so that at present we can carry on with half our power, but will that be enough to bear us safely past the German trenches ?

If we had a rev.-counter to tell us the number of revolutions per minute that the propeller is doing, we should be in a better position to ascertain the cause of the trouble. But as matters stand, our only adviser is the altimeter, the indicator of which glides slowly but inexorably to the left.

Suddenly something begins to whirl in my head. " Good Lord ! " I groan inwardly, " I haven't been looking out for any enemy machines ! " I turn round and search the horizon ; luckily there is not a plane to be seen anywhere. We should be in evil case if we had to fight with a coughing engine.

On the road from Châlons to Rheims a transport column jogs its way towards the front, preceded by two horsemen—probably *M. le Capitaine* and his bugler. Despite our precarious plight I cannot help a hearty laugh when suddenly great clouds of dust whirl up into the air. The drivers have noticed our descent and put their horses into a gallop to escape from our bombs. The two in front must be going at a good rate because their distance from the foremost wagon increases perceptibly. They guess rightly that if the *Boche* drops a bomb he will unload it on the main column rather than the couple of solitary horsemen. If only they knew that we are in a far tighter corner than they are !

*Bonjour, messieurs !*

But the incident does more than cheer me up ; it reminds me that we still have our two bombs on board. Involuntarily my hand feels for the lever. Away with those bombs ; they are only useless ballast now ! Chuck them anywhere ! But I cannot make up my mind to waste those two lovely twenty-kilo chaps by shoving them down to tear two big holes in a French field. No, they will have to do a bit more damage than that !

One thing is, however, clear. If we cause a number of casualties and then have to land anywhere in the neighbourhood of the infuriated survivors, we shall be shot at once or knocked on the head. All the same, I'll risk it.

I peer out in the direction of the front. We shall be flying over a camp in a moment, and that's the place for my bombs. I'll have that satisfaction, at least.

Then I search the horizon again for hostile aircraft. Not a Frenchman to be seen.

What's our present height? The slim indicator is just moving on to the thick 2—now there's a small space between—which gets bigger—the indicator is going back to 1900.

If the engine goes dead here, as it may at any moment, we can glide a distance five times our height—that is to say, just under ten kilometres. And we are still twelve kilometres behind the front! In my trouser pocket my fingers feel for the box of incendiary matches. I carefully extract it. Seven matches it contains; I stick them in the right pocket of my leather jacket. In the left I place the machine gun's screwdriver, which I shall jab through the thin tin side of the emergency tank when we land. Then light a match—hold it to the spurting benzine—and the Frenchies will have little joy or profit in the prize that falls unsought into their hands.

Ah, there comes our target! I reflect a moment —as we are only 1700 metres up, we don't need to allow much for deflection—hand on lever—wait a moment—not yet—that's it—now! "Bump! Bump!"

I watch the falling bombs until they disappear from my view. Two great clouds of debris rise up —one before and—hurrah! the other bang in the middle of the camp. I've got something to show for my trouble now, whatever happens afterwards!

Another pleasant little surprise for me! Squinting out through the wires I see a French captive balloon. It is the first outpost of the near front, and my spirits rise as I see the ground squad tugging frantically to haul down their fat cigar-shaped envelope to protect it from the *avion boche*. The lower it sinks, the higher rises my pride. (See sketch at chapter-heading.)

I point the ground squad out to my good Take to cheer him up. But he bestows only the merest cursory glance at their efforts and then turns to stare at me with sorrowful eyes.

"We're jolly fine fellows!" I shout, giving him a jovial nudge. And so, despite our hell of a mess, I wring a laugh out of the despondent Take, who is amused at my arrogance.

After crawling along at a snail's pace for a few more minutes, with our hearts in our mouths, we cross the trenches of the French second line.

We have done the trick, for now we can get back in a glide even if the engine goes dead this very moment.

Whoof! Whoof!

The first shells from the Archie of the front.

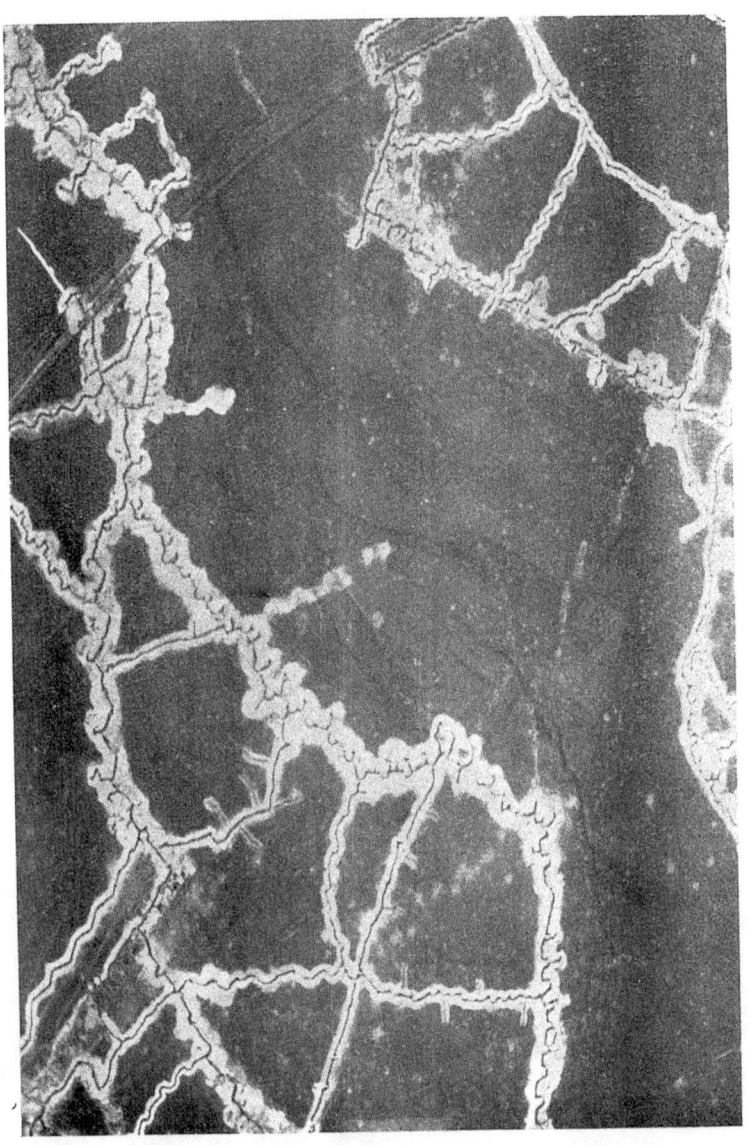

TRENCHES AND NO MAN'S LAND

*Facing page 92*

But what do we care about them now we know we've pulled it off?

Ambition prompts a battery of field artillery to join in. They want to have the joy of peppering the boches as well as their colleagues of the *canons spéciaux*,[1] and so a keen match takes place. Right and left of us the grey shells burst, always four at a time. The nearest are somewhere within a thousand metres of us.

"Look behind you!" I shout to Engmann, pointing to the new field battery, whose shells are bursting four kilometres away. "Lovely shooting, isn't it?"

While we glide down over No Man's Land, Engmann rouses the furious gunners to white-hot excitement by putting the machine into a vigorous right-hand turn. Soon afterwards he makes a good landing on No. 10's aerodrome at Merland-Ferme.

When we have mastered our laughter sufficiently to climb out of the cockpit, I pinch the lobe of Engmann's ear and whisper softly: "Well, I'm damned!"

---

[1] *Canons spéciaux.* French name for anti-aircraft artillery.

# CHAPTER VIII

### THIRTY DEGREES BELOW

"KNOORRPS! Knoorrps! Knoorpps!" sighed the snow under our feet.

"A nice job to-day," opined Engmann. "Three hours at 4,000 in this hellish cold, burr!"

The machine stood before the hangar's door. Lance-Corporal Schulz was bringing hot water in two steaming buckets. To prevent it freezing, it had to be mixed with glycerine before it could be poured in. (See sketch at chapter heading.)

Meanwhile we finished dressing ourselves. We looked like a couple of Arctic explorers: thickly-padded over-trousers, fur-lined boots reaching to above the knee, fur-lined waistcoats, leather jackets, thick woollen scarves, fur caps, crash helmets, silk gloves, fur-lined leather gloves.

Finally our faces were smeared with thick slabs of grease. Only our lips and eyes were spared this anointment. Then we were ready.

I could not help laughing when I stared at myself in the mirror. Not exactly the sort of face to kiss. Engmann stared at me reflectively.

"We ought to be photographed in this get-up," he remarked.

"But, my dear Take! Before a flight?"

"No, no, no!" he protested in dismay. "Not that I'm superstitious, of course. But if you should happen to be hit to-day, then of course——"

I clapped a hand in front of his mouth.

"Shut your mug; it's making a draught!" I interrupted him. "Of course, the only reason why we decline to be snapped before our start is that we do not wish to cause any unnecessary delay."

Then I stumped up to the bus on my elephantine legs and climbed in. While Engmann gave the engine its trial run, I hunched my shoulders, shivering at the draught. Oh, damn and damn again, what a hell of a cold! The wind from the propeller groaned as it set the little snow crystals madly dancing in the air. More and more of them it whirled off the ground until at last there was a naked patch of brown grass. The sun sparkled on a million crystal facets and conjured up a rainbow in the air. Splendidly and exquisitely beautiful, if only it wasn't so damnably cold!

Then the engine insulted my ears by stuttering and refusing to take its revs. At last Engmann cut off the ignition.

"What's up?" I asked.

The flight sergeant shrugged his shoulders.

"Water-pump and carburetter frozen, sir. Will have to be thawed out slowly."

"How long?"

"Ten minutes."

So I climbed out of my cockpit to stretch my legs a bit. After a quarter of an hour the engine was working again and we rolled slowly to the end of the long fairway that the starting squad had made at dawn by shovelling away the snow. I fastened on my winter goggles, to which were attached shapeless flaps of untanned leather to protect my face from freezing and pushed the loose end of my scarf into my mouth.

"Right away!"

.   .   .   .

Half an hour in the air.

Lord, it is brutally cold! There's a draught finding its way in through the bomb-hole, and it's biting me like a mad dog! Hell alone knows how it can penetrate through my leather outer clothing and all the layers underneath! But it does, and it's freezing my body to ice. The process begun at my toes, then the cold crept slowly up to my knees, gave me pins and needles in my thighs, and now I'm numb up to my arms. I mark time with my toes to prevent them getting frost-bitten, wriggle about on my seat to drive the chill out of my backbone and pound my thighs with clenched fists until they warm up again.

Meanwhile my breath has emerged from under my leather flaps and settled down on my goggles,

## THIRTY DEGREES BELOW

where it has frozen stiff. I remove the goggles and scratch the ice off them with the screw-driver. A bad business!

While I stamp about in the cockpit like a polar bear gone off his head, my eye falls by chance on the compass. It is coated with a layer of ice, which is luckily thin and smooth enough for me to see through it. Most compasses have a needle pivoted on a vertical axis, but ours consists of a magnetized card or "rose," floating in a bowl of glycerine. Although this liquid is noted for its extraordinarily low freezing point, to-day's temperature is evidently too cold for it, for the north point on the card points straight ahead, whereas we are steering due east.

The machine is climbing, and when Engmann flies a wide spiral, the card makes no motion at all.

A blessing that the sky is clear! If we had to fly through thick clouds with a frozen compass—no, no thank you!

.    .

We fly over the trenches.

Archie's first effort comes fairly near us. I laugh grimly. Oh, what a day! And yet there is a good side to the bursting shells that set our ears buzzing and the shrapnel bullets that whizz past our cockpit, for—strangely enough!—they drive out of my leather jacket the cold that chilled my warm blood and was in process of eating the flesh off my bones. Yes, better still! one shell that comes devilishly near gives me a hot feeling down the spine. But the further we leave Archie behind us, the fiercer the frost assails my body again.

I rise and thump my arms against my body. Then I mark time with my feet. A temporary relief, at least, and thereupon I look down to right and left and make observations. Finally I search the air for enemy machines. Not a plane in sight! Well, that's another blessing we get from this cold weather.

From St. Hilaire junction a south-bound train steams out. Its smoke is a silvery white, sharply outlined in the frozen air. With much laborious fumbling I extract a pencil from my jacket's pocket and, holding it between my fingers like a long cigar, I contrive to note the train on my map.

Then I mark time with my feet again, clap my hands and press my ears against my head.

Châlons station rolls up. As I have to take a photo of it, I extract my camera from its rack. I have only to get the shutter away from the plate, but can I do it? My bearlike paws cannot grasp the little tag on the sheath. I quickly pull the button of my right hand glove apart with my teeth, wedge my fingers between my knees, and tear off both the leather and the silk gloves.

Then I lean overboard—focus—click! done!

I needed barely three seconds for the operation. But when I try to replace the shutter, it can't be done. My hand is frozen as stiff as a post. I push the camera away, and try to rub some warmth into my blue fingers with my knees.

## THIRTY DEGREES BELOW

As that does not do much good, I let go of the scarf end that I have kept in my mouth and endeavour to drive the frost out of my hand with my breath. Very gradually the blood warms up ; on with the two gloves again, before the hand has time to freeze once more, and then we'll have another shot at getting the aluminium shutter in position.

When you're flying, the worst thing about a severe frost is the fact that the wind from the propeller blows away the protective layer of vapour that the warmth of your blood puts out around your body. A few days later I saw on the hand of an incautious colleague the effect of this extreme cold on any part of the body that is left exposed for only a few minutes. The frostbites resembled severe burns. (See Illustration No. 9.)

Then I get a shock. Whoof! whoof!

Shell fire! I search the air and bend overboard. Not a sign of a shellburst to be seen anywhere. Funny! There it goes again—whoof! and quite near too!

At last I find the key of the riddle. That's not Archie—it's my scarf! The end I kept in my mouth for some time was wet with my breath, and now the cold, cutting air has frozen it stiff. It was as hard as a board when the propeller wind caught it and smacked it against my helmet with a noise that sounded exactly like a bursting shell.

. . .

I take another five photos.

They are well worth the trouble to-day. The

fresh-fallen snow shows up everything. It enables my camera to see through the pine woods that usually camouflage certain camps. (See Illustration No. 10.) It also reveals as black lines carved into the white surfaces the paths trodden by feet, hooves and wheels, and so tells us which buildings are occupied. (See Illustration No. 11.)

What a pity I did not bring along a few more plates!

When I have done the last one, I make a determined effort to force the shutter over the exposed plate. But my bent fingers cannot fit it into the narrow slit, and—smack! the whirlwind has torn it out of my numb hand. I gaze after it and see the wind hurling it earthwards; every time that the broad side is turned towards me, it gleams mockingly in the sunlight.

What's gone is lost! We must make a quick curve so that I can get another photo. The plate is spoilt; I cannot leave it in the camera because I have other positions to photograph.

I have just done it, when suddenly something gleaming comes into my vision. A French Spad single-seater is heading for us; it whirls past below.

More trouble!

And yet—strange as it may seem—a wave of warmth appears to surge through my body again.

In a twinkling I swing the machine gun round. The Frenchman does not seem to have manœuvred himself into the right position, for he circles round and comes at us again from his first direction.

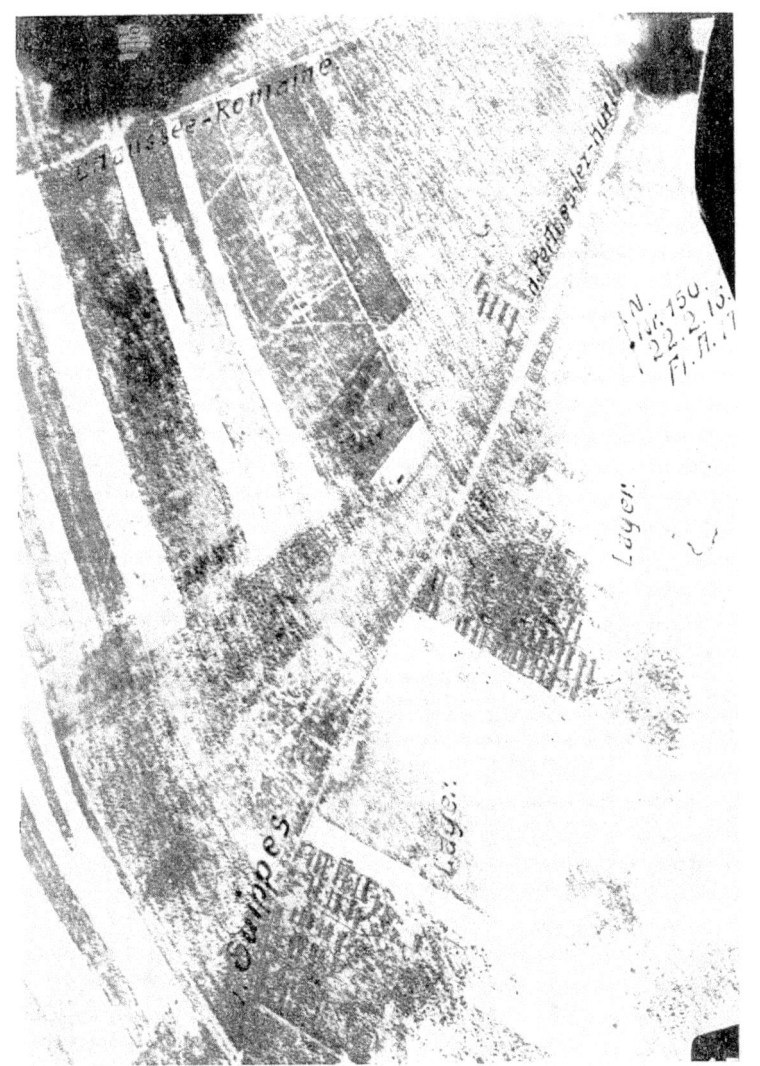

A French Camp in the Pine Woods

# THIRTY DEGREES BELOW

Wait a moment, though—he's in a turn—now he's climbing—he's as high as we are—no, he's above us—and he's going to dive on us. Eight hundred metres away, I judge him; I'll wait till he's a bit nearer. Mere waste of ammunition to shoot too soon!

Having examined the landscape once more and exposed my last plate, I sight him at 400 metres. But he does not shoot—thinks he's going to spring a surprise on us, does my fine gentleman. Sorry, I must disappoint him!

Tack—tack—tack—tack—tack! I rattle away at him on my machine gun.

Automatically he swerves slightly. When I have him sighted once more, I press the button—but my gun remains silent.

A jam!

While I push the catch forward and tug at the belt, his bullets begin to hail on us. Engmann goes into a turn to dodge the deadly shower.

But now I am on my mark again. Tack—tack—tack!

Three shots I fire—then the gun is silent again. Another jam. Ah, I think I can guess the trouble. The belt is frozen stiff—lost all its flexibility.

I release the catch again and push it along. Then I sight the Spad once more—sight him beautifully!

Seven—eight shots—then another jam! And meanwhile the rattle from the machine gun of the ever-approaching Frenchman makes a most painful impression upon my ears.

So ho, now we've got our gun working again! Hurrah! We've let off twenty shots without a jam. My opponent turns slightly, but returns to the attack immediately.

Tack?

Not one shot this time—enough to drive a fellow crazy! Engmann guesses the trouble at once and goes into a series of hair-raising turns. Good for us—the Frenchman doesn't hit us once. I anchor my right leg to the leg of my tip-up seat to keep myself from being thrown out in these devilish turns. "Home again!" I nod to Engmann in the mirror.

Once again I try to release the catch in order to remove the jam. I cannot manage it. I pull my right glove off and have another shot at it. This time I succeed, although I leave some shreds of skin sticking to the frozen metal.

Consequently I am able to put in a series of shots on the Spad. The pilot appears to be a bit puzzled; no doubt he thought we were easy fruit for him with all those jams, and now my machine gun is spitting out a fresh stream of bullets. He goes into a steep right-hand turn and makes off.

I have not the least objection, for the very next moment I get another jam—my eighth!

.   .   .

After landing, we have ourselves photographed as arctic explorers. When some little while later I remove the grease from my face, my

11 THE ROADS LEADING TO THE CAMP REVEALED BY TRACKS IN THE SNOW

*Facing page* 102

mirror shows me a countenance that seems to glow with radiant health.

"No frostbites, at least!" I think—or rather, thought. For that same afternoon my face blazes like a red poppy, and when I enter the messroom for dinner in the evening, I resemble a full-blown rose of summer. Chin, upper lip, nose and both cheeks have succumbed to the frost.

Insult is added to injury, for as I make my entrance, everyone—from the captain down to little Beckmann who only joined us a couple of days ago—is grinning.

"If I were your commanding officer," scoffed Fischer, "I'd courtmartial you for wilful self-mutilation." And Captain Mohr turned his face from me with something approaching a shudder.

"No, you're not exactly a pretty child!" he observed.

And that was my country's thanks to me.

## CHAPTER IX

### VISITING CARDS

WE were reading the newspapers which had just arrived one evening after dinner. Suddenly 2nd Lieutenant Holzhausen laughed loudly. "You can say what you like, but the French understand the gentle art of advertisement perfectly. Here's their latest: 'Arm in arm with our Russian brethren against the German barbarians! *Vive la sainte Alliance!*' Here, read it for yourself, right upper column!" I took the paper from him.

"THE RUSSIANS LAND IN MARSEILLES.

"W.T.B. Geneva, May 5th, 1916. (From our special correspondent.)

" The *Journal de Genève* writes : The Russians who have recently landed in Marseilles do not appear to be more than 900 strong. As they are without arms or equipment, it will be some time yet before they can proceed to the front."

Meditatively I passed the paper back to Holzhausen. " Yes, the French know how to blow their own trumpets. *C'est le ton qui fait la musique.* And, by the way, I could do with a few prisoners to put some cinders down on the road to the aerodrome."

" Granted," said Holzhausen. " The skin of the first Russian bear we catch is yours."

. . . . .

During the next few days we scanned the papers eagerly for further news of our Russians, but the sources of information were meagre. In an illustrated weekly we found a picture of their landing in Marseilles.

In *Je sais tout* [1] M. Victor Forbin gave a detailed account of the journey of these brothers in arms. On February 26th they embarked in Vladivostock on the French steamboats, " Latouche-Tréville " and " Himalaya." Protection against submarines was undertaken by Japanese torpedo boats and later by a British squadron.

. . . . .

A week later Holzhausen buttonholed me again. " Here's the very latest about our moujiks," he

---

[1] *Je sais tout*, = " I know everything." The title of a well-known French magazine.

announced, " it was in yesterday's paper. Prince Somebody or other . . . unpronounceable name ending in ' off ' . . . attached to the Russian Embassy in Paris, paid a visit to the Russian troops quartered in France. And where do you think they now are ? "

" Not the least idea ! "

" In Mailly camp."

I pondered. Mailly—Mailly—where was Mailly ? And then I remembered something that I had read in the *Figaro* a few months previously. In February, General Pétain had commandeered a lot of motor-cars and loaded them up with the 21st Army Corps, which had been withdrawn to Mailly. Then he sent them off to Verdun, where the situation was critical.

In that case the camp was somewhere not far behind the Marne. I soon found it on the map . . . barely more than 100 kilometres from our aerodrome.

. .

The following morning I was on the dawn patrol. Over breakfast I told Engmann of the previous night's conversation. He gave me a knowing wink.

" Got your visiting card ready ? " he inquired.

We understood one another. If the Russians had already been a whole week in Mailly camp, then it was high time for us to welcome them to the Western Front. I nodded joyfully to Take.

" A fifty-kilo egg," I suggested. " Because of the good moral effect it will produce."

. . . . .

At 3.45 a.m. we start off with full tanks and our fifty-kilo bomb. But as soon as we are in the air, I find I have a sin of omission on my conscience: I have forgotten to warn our Archie at Givry. We must quickly send them a message with our signalling pistol: " Dear friend, please don't shoot at us if you can possibly help it."

The early dawn of the coming day is not yet strong enough to compete with the mild moonbeams. I am reminded of Goethe's " Ode to the Moon " :

" Again thou fillest hill and dale."

Yes, " fillest " is good . . . quite a good phrase.

The tender flowers of romance do not grow in the harsh soil of No. 17's aerodrome, and yet I feel my heart enchanted by the magic of this wondrous moonlit night in spite of my fifty-kilo bomb and the two machine guns we are now carrying.

I look back. The regulation flare that my mechanics have lit on our aerodrome is still visible as a red pinpoint of light that speeds us on our way. Then I observe that No. 22 Squadron seems to be busy this morning; at Lessingcourt aerodrome they have marked out the landing " T " with five white lights.

Instead of climbing we save time by flying a direct course to the front, and shortly after 4 a.m. we cross the trenches near Rheims at a height of 1500 metres. The town still lies wrapped in slumber; the only light I can see is one that flickers somewhere near the station.

We go on past the *Forêt de Rheims*, making good progress against the light southerly breeze. We would not have minded a stiff headwind to-day, for the time it would have lost us on the outward journey we should have made up on our return when we had it behind us. The homeward trip always seems the longest part of the business, especially when there are French aeroplanes knocking around and wanting to fight us.

Suddenly I get an unpleasant shock: hostile aircraft are about already! The moon gleams treacherously on the varnished fabric of their wings. But the next moment I breathe freely again. A false alarm: it was only the reflection of the moonbeams on a small pond.

With mind at ease once more I continue my observations. A long trail of smoke proclaims the approach of the first train. I take up my binoculars. The train passes a level-crossing which gives me a convenient chance to count the number of its trucks. I jot down fifty on my map.

To my left lies Epernay station. The arc lamps are provided with big shades to mask them from observation by our aircraft, but the circles of light they throw on the ground below are traitors that reveal them to me.

Hallo, there's a searchlight! I crouch on my seat . . . no, another false alarm. Merely the reflection of moonlight on the water again!

A memory of schoolboy days flits into my brain. We used to love to flash our pocket-lamps in the faces of peaceful passers-by—or, better still, one of our masters. Now twice in quick succession I have been the victim of two such practical jokes played on me by the moonbeams.

A few minutes later we fly over the Marne, but to-day we do not go into the usual left-hand turn. We fly straight ahead on a southerly course. It is unfamiliar territory to us, but as the light grows stronger every minute, it is not so difficult to find our way. Already I can read my map without any assistance from my torch. The railway lines seem to run fairly straight ahead, with very few bends; we can feel our way along them. The roads intersecting the railway tell me that I am going in the right direction. That little town down there, bedded in its vineyards, is Vertus where they grow grapes for the good brands of champagne. I cannot resist a smile; only 4000 metres beneath me lie the cellars where the thick-gold-necked bottles are stored—so near and yet so far!

Fère-Champenoise. At the station the railway lines that hitherto have guided us so faithfully swing off at a right-angle to our course. I examine the station with my glasses; very little traffic about, it seems.

The road confirms my identification of the place. Three main roads cross here, says my map, and I can see them radiating from the little town in their various directions. Here we turn off eastward, following the long, straight road to Sommesous. The name conjures up sad memories. This was the place where our forward movement ended in 1914—there the incomprehensible order to retreat reached us—the fortunes of war turned—for the French began "the miracle of the Marne."

Meanwhile the day has dawned. It is now clear enough for me to survey the landscape, so that I need no longer hug the main lines of traffic. I therefore signal Engmann to leave the high road running south-eastward and follow the one that leads direct to Mailly.

When he has put the machine into the new course, I peer out past the engine.

Ah, there is the camp! I see a long, quadrangular block, enclosing many little rectangular smears, which are the barracks. Behind it, to the right, there is a cluster of stone buildings, which must be the offices and officers' quarters. A tempting target, but as I have only one bomb to drop, I must not let myself be enticed to experiment with it.

With a whack on the shoulder I direct Engmann to fly diagonally across the camp. "Knack" says the safety-catch of the bomb-rack as I release it, and the lever answers "knack." I grip the handle and lean overboard. Yes, there are signs of life below; from two—no, three—barracks a delicate, blue stream of smoke curls upwards. From the kitchens, probably.

Now we are at the right spot. Just before we reach the foremost building I pull the lever and lean out to look. After a couple of zigzag motions the monster bomb shoots downward like an arrow from the bow.

I hold my breath and wait. Twenty seconds. It ought to be down by now. Oh Lord, what a long business it is! Have I missed? My eyes search the camp. Where is it, where, where, where? Yes, look there, a flash—and then a huge cloud of smoke—bang in the middle of the camp!
Ah!
I take a hurried snapshot, grin at good old Take in the mirror and clap my hands. He understands and nods back at me vigorously. When I turn round again, I see that two barracks are on fire. That too! Thick swaths of smoke are swirling about the camp.

I signal Engmann into a turn, so that he can see and rejoice over our bomb's success. After waving his right hand at me to show his recognition, he turns again and steers northward.

While I am still staring at the burning barracks, a bright idea strikes me. I hastily whack Engmann's left shoulder: half-left turn! I mean to keep him steering north-west until we have passed Sommesous and can no longer be seen or heard by the inmates of the camp; then we must turn sharp to north-east. Why? Because I imagine the French single-seaters will be waiting for us somewhere near Rheims—i.e., fairly well to north-westward.

For now we have the worst part of the business before us. The men down below will be on the telephone to the various aerodromes—they will have informed the people at the front about our attack on their camp—all the single-seaters will be hunting us down. The same thought must have occurred to Engmann because he peers out carefully to right and left of him.

Two trains creep along to the front, from which another is returning. I jot all three down on my map and then stare out ahead of me again. Far away in the morning haze I can see the Marne. Engmann shrugs his shoulders and points to the river. I lean over to him and shout in his ear through the roar of the engine: "Marne!"

He nods and wriggles on his seat to show how delighted he is that we have now a goodly part of the way behind us.

Ever nearer comes the broad band of the river that reflects the grey light of morning. For the last time I look back at Mailly, where I see the red flames still gleaming through the clouds of smoke.

We leave Châlons on our left. And now for the last act of our show, though what a pity I cannot tell whether it will be a tragedy or a comedy. The decision on this point rests with ourselves and the machine guns of the fast French scouts whom we may shortly expect to find swarming up to us. Uneasily I comb the air, and uneasily Engmann wriggles about on his seat.

Meanwhile the sun has risen above the strip of haze that veils the horizon and bathes our bird in a wondrous red that we detest because it will betray us to the enemy. But now we are only ten kilometres from the front, and every second brings us nearer to our comrades.

Hello, there's the first Archie! High above us

—a pretty little white, cottonwool cloud! And another the next moment! The altimeter shows our height as 4,000, but those shots must be bursting a good thousand higher.

And here's the first Nieuport. Coming from the left. He's still below us, but he's climbing like mad. And—oh, curse it!—there's another close behind him, and a third over there, to the right, followed by Nos. 4 and 5—some distance behind them a sixth—and, oh heavens! more of them behind him! There must be at least ten of them, and they're after us like Satan's host after a lost soul. (See sketch at chapter heading.)

Brrr! What a pack of hounds!

I make a lightning calculation of the respective distances between ourselves and the nearest opponent and between ourselves and the front. Then I breathed a hearty sigh of relief—you are too late, *Messieurs*.

They have made too wide a sweep to westward. This is no matter of chance, but implies the success of my trick. They fell into my trap when I steered a north-west course after dropping my bomb and then turned sharply to the north-east later.

Now we come under the fire of Archie at the front, and when our foremost pursuer sees the first shell burst between him and us, he gives up the chase and sheers away to southward. The others follow him; despite their handicap of three-quarters of an hour, they have not managed to catch us.

We grin at one another in the mirror. Got away with it!

In my joyous arrogance I signal Engmann to circle round in the midst of their fire. This round, which finishes our long and thrilling homeward flight, seems to me to bear some resemblance to the finish of a lively little porker—i.e., his neat little curly tail. An apt comparison, for, like the students in Auerbach's cellar

"As 'twere five hundred hogs we feel
So cannibalic jolly!"

Then, as we bank over onto our right wing and see the white shell-bursts whirling madly round us, I picture myself as a step-dancer pirouetting about among a lot of broken eggs.

Back over the front we go! Engmann throttles down and puts the machine into a glide that will just bring it to Attigny aerodrome. Then we stretch our limbs and begin to appreciate the beauty of the young May morning. As our tension has been over-long to-day, we have to let off steam. We sing, whistle and yell our war-whoop into the air around us.

Hoi-ee-ee-ee-ee!

The earth's a jolly old place, after all! Dear old Take is in a romantic mood. He points to the Argonne wood, where the new foliage shows like a smile of spring against the dark evergreen of the pines, nods his recognition of its beauty and turns round to me:

"Lovely, isn't it?"

I laugh heartily at his sudden awakening to the glories of Nature and return the compliment by waving my hand towards the Aisne valley where the morning mist hangs like an exquisitely delicate veil about the trees and bushes that gain a wondrous enhancement of form by the long shadows they throw.

. . . . .

I was very pleased with our friendly call on the Russians, but there is always a fly in the ointment. When I laid my report before my C.O. he was as delighted as we were that the business had gone off well.

"But what about the photos?" he asked.

I shrugged my shoulders.

"Messed up, unfortunately. The morning light was too weak. I used an open lens and one one-hundred-and-fiftieth of a second's exposure, but there was practically nothing on the plates."

Captain Mohr pushed out his lower lip sympathetically. "What a pity we can't show H.Q. a picture of the business!"

Several days later our single-seaters shot down a French scout, the pilot of which had something to say about our raid on Mailly camp.

"*Ah, nous étions pleins d'admiration!* And it gave us a lot of trouble, too, because all our scouts were pushed up into the air to try to catch the bomb-throwers. But we couldn't come near them, and got a devil of a ticking off about it."

"And what damage did the bomb do?"

The Frenchman laughed. "None at all, luckily. It burst outside the camp."

Captain Mohr pulled a long face when he reported this to me, but I was able to set his mind at ease.

"Naturally the fellow told you a barefaced lie," I assured him. "I saw the bomb burst bang in the middle of the camp. And in any case they'll have to send those Russians to the front sooner or later, and the first of them we take prisoner will confirm my report."

I tried to appear casual about the affair, but inwardly I seethed with hatred against the patriotic Frenchman whose deliberate lie had injured my reputation. Though none of my messmates cast any doubts on the accuracy of my statement, I could not ascertain what they really thought. After all, it was only one man's word against another's.

.  .  .  .

Luckily I was not kept waiting until we could catch our first Russian, because the *Frankfurter Zeitung* furnished timely confirmation of my success.

"Bern, May 20th. (Priv.-Tel.) Yesterday at dawn a German aeroplane flew over Mailly camp where the Russian troops are undergoing training. A bomb was dropped, which burst and caused considerable damage."

So I was able to lift up my head once more.

Two stitches are better than one. After the Russians had been put in the line somewhere near Tahure, some prisoners were captured in a trench raid and sent to our intelligence officer.

They confirmed the report in the press. In addition to the " considerable damage " (two barracks burnt to the ground) the Russians sustained numerous casualties.

I rejoiced heartily—not at any loss of life my success had caused, but over the fact that my report was confirmed.

## CHAPTER X

### SAVE ME FROM MY FRIENDS

TAKE ENGMANN and I were assigned to the second patrol and wanted to start immediately after lunch. But we had to wait because the sky had clouded over during the meal and did not clear up until late in the afternoon.

. . . . .

A wonderful flight into the gloaming lies before us. Visibility is good, and better still is the strong west wind at our backs that bowls us merrily along.

All the same, I do not feel comfortable. Throughout the trip we have not seen the shell of a single Archie, and we have had no fights in the air—as a matter of fact, we have not seen a single French machine up aloft. This excess of twilight peace disturbs me.

High time for me to find a resting-place for my two twenty-kilo bombs. I decide to bestow them on Ste Ménehould station, which we have neglected for some time. But when I look out ahead, I pull a long face: clouds are rolling up again.

The first wisps of cloud meet us over Valmy. They grow and grow, until suddenly we find ourselves flying over a thick blanket. Here and there a dark patch shows us a little piece of mother earth beneath us. We have been lucky to get through all our job except those two bombs for Ste Ménehould.

What am I going to do with those eggs? The simplest solution would be just to drop them out through the clouds, but I cannot bring myself to perpetrate such sinful waste. I would rather take them back to Attigny, and even though we shall have to land at night, Engmann has never had a crash—and the firing pins of the bombs are secured with a safety device.

Nothing more to reconnoitre, so we'd better go home. But first we must get our bearings so that we can fly back over the clouds. Where's the sun? Ah, over yonder there's a red arch in the clouds, and I can see an orange that is getting paler every moment. That is north-west, then.

The moon is up as well. I can see her in the north-east, right opposite the setting sun.

In addition to these two guides I have my compass, the needle of which confirms the information supplied to me by the forces of Nature. So I whack Engmann to the north and give him an extra biff on his helmet.

"Prolonged glide!" it signifies.

We drop earthwards, doing 800 revs. To-day we can risk it, although we are still ten kilometres off the front. But we are hardly likely to meet any hostile aircraft, while the clouds will protect us from Archie. Before we touch even their topmost layer, we ought to have glided a good way beyond the trenches.

3,000—2,500—2000—— Still high above the clouds!

The darkness rushes on us in leaps and bounds. Up aloft we were still able to distinguish a faint glow from the setting sun, but now we are sinking as well as the sun. Night comes on us without any twilight, as it comes in the tropics—a procedure so unusual for us denizens of a northern clime that it makes me a bit uneasy. Engmann is also feeling worried and wants to open his engine out again. But I lay my arm on his arm as it feels for the switch.

"Drop down to the clouds!" I instruct him.

Deeper and deeper we glide. Now the last shimmer of sunshine has vanished, but the silvery moonlight increases in brightness as it streams up over the white clouds beneath our feet. The nearer we come to the cloud bank, the longer becomes my face. That is no layer of stratus clouds, but a mass of cumuli! Luckily for us, it is not so big because the altimeter registers only 1,500 metres when we touch its highest point. As we glide ever deeper, clumps of them rise up from the white mass that looked exactly like a snowfield when viewed from above. This moon-drenched cloud landscape may look beautiful, but the idea of having to push our way through it makes me shudder. I have got to make up my mind to it, however, as we cannot very well spend the night up here.

Question : Have we flown over the front ?
Answer : Yes.
Deduction : Down with our machine !

That does not mean that we are going to push our heads into the wall of clouds ; no, we shall feel our way with the machine's nose along the mountain mass until we find a chance to thrust ourselves through the floor of one of its valleys. Our easiest way down is to break through the thinnest layer we can find.

Over there I see a wide bowl, and the darkness in its depths looks promising. If it is not caused by shadows, it signifies a hole in the clouds through which we have a clear passage to the ground beneath.

So I instruct Engmann accordingly, and we glide into the bowl to descend in spiral turns along its inner walling. The deeper we descend, the higher seem the domes and pinnacles of cloud that tower above us on every side.

Now the moon dips below a battlement of clouds, and only one solitary, sympathetic little star flickers almost vertically above us. For a while we fly onward through blue darkness, but at last the moon appears on the farther side of the battlements.

We continue to glide down. Our lunar friend and guide is swallowed up by a cloud, but it is only a thin one because it allows a pale, rayless disc to shimmer through it. Then the veil grows thicker, until it completely hides the moon from us.

One always feels a fool when one has to push one's way through a cloud layer at night and does not know how thick it is. And then, into a corner of my brain creeps the disturbing thought: " Are we quite sure we are not still flying over the enemy's territory ? "

That is still a matter of uncertainty. The only certain thing is that when we get through the clouds we shall be flying in night—starless night.

Through the gloom of the night we are gliding into Nirvana. I rise and bend over to the pilot's seat, where, holding on with both hands to the struts of the centre section, I stare across Take's shoulders at the rev.-counter. The thick radium indicator wobbles uneasily between 400 and 700. The seconds drag slowly on like falling drops of thick syrup ; already we have spent half a minute cut off from both heaven and earth, and then— oh joy !—we have our first glimpse of the earth when a river reflects its pallid surface up to us. Our sense of balance is born anew—ah ! A few seconds later we are wrapped in clouds again, but they do not matter. They are only miserable shreds and patches through which we shall soon push our way.

Down below we are in pitch-black night, but as soon as our eyes grow accustomed to the gloom, we identify a sack of clouds hanging below the general level and dodge it. We fly below it at 600 metres. Now to get our bearings!

A quick glance round satisfies me that we are flying over German territory, and I welcome the news with a deep sigh of relief. I presumed all along that this was the case, but certainty is better than presumption.

Over there where I can see the flashes, where rockets rise vertically in the air, only to sink in gleaming trails to earth and slowly die, yes, over there is the front.

Then I realize another fact which is not so pleasant. The river that greeted us as earth's first messenger must be the Meuse, so that the drum fire on our left must come from the northern front of Verdun!

In the course of our journey above the clouds the strong west-wind has therefore drifted us thirty kilometres too far eastward. Or, rather, it would be more truthful to say that the clouds and wind are not responsible, but that Herr Heydemarck made a big mistake in his calculations. I decide to break the bad news gently to Engmann so as not to alarm him unnecessarily.

"We're a bit too far to the right," I tell him. "Better go back those few kilometres to the front so that we can feel our way home along it."

Take nods and starts his engine again. "Home!" chants joyfully its iron lay, though it will be a good half-hour before we can get back against that strong headwind. Never mind! The artillery flashes and the rockets will be infallible guides that are bound to lead us home without further mishap—at least, so I suppose in my ignorance.

We turn to face the strong west wind and fight our way laboriously back to the front. Seen from afar, it resembles a road illumined by a multitude of arc-lamps, in which the headlights of a thousand cars shine, disappear and shine again in new positions. But in the lurid gleam of the falling rockets we recognize the truth: here is the street of death. To right and left, as far as our eyes can reach, we see the white masses of chalk from which the soil has been stripped. Mother Earth bleeds from a thousand wounds which have not healed for years because every fresh shell and every new mine tears them open again.

At a height of 600 metres we fly along this ghastly road.

Suddenly Engmann pulls back the switch.

" Benzine nearly finished ! " he announces.

That does not worry me greatly because the emergency tank contains benzine for twenty minutes. That will suffice. I bend over to him: " Take care to switch on the emergency tank at the right moment so that the propeller doesn't stop."

Plan of action : To hug the front until we reach the high road that intersects the trenches at Ville-sur-Tourbe, and then follow it until it leads us to Attigny. With the miserable pittance of benzine that remains to us, we cannot afford the luxury of missing our way again. Therefore I must keep to the safe roads, even if they lead me a longer way round. Under no circumstances must I attempt a cross-country route to Attigny. No—never!

But: " never " is a word one must never use.

To our right, somewhere out on the far horizon, a fiery ball rises into the air, bursts and sends a shower of sparks to earth. That is a fog-bomb! When its bright glow has faded away, I see clearly a green and two red lights; my heart welcomes them even before my reason grasps their significance. They gleam from our aerodrome—over there is Attigny, with our comrades who are getting anxious about us and so call to us over the space of forty kilometres.

The next moment Engmann gets a whack on his right shoulder: " Make for those coloured lights." He quickly understands and steers towards them.

And despite the darkness of the night our hearts are full of sunshine.

.   .

Three minutes later Take turns round to me: " I'm switching on the emergency tank."

I calculate. We shall just get home. A good thing I saw that fog-bomb, as we could never have managed the longer way round by Ville-sur-Tourbe. Another bit of luck!

But suddenly I see two sharp flashes gleam beneath us. Ten seconds later two shells burst above us.

We are being peppered by our own Archie!

The flashes of those first two shells are signals for an indiscriminate bombardment. All around us for miles fire is belched into the night, all around us in the air burst shells and shrapnels. Out with my light-pistol!

The German identification signal is a ball of light that bursts after a few seconds in the air and pours out a shower of white stars. These star-shells, which consist of tin capsules filled with magnesium, produce a strong light and also a most intensive heat, so that one has to handle a loaded light-pistol more carefully than a raw egg. Once such a pistol went off by accident in an airman's hands, with the result that its missile bored its way through the cockpit, which it set on fire. The machine went down in flames, and after the sad accident orders were given to keep the pistol's barrel in a special hole in the cockpit.

Just as I touch the pistol's butt-end, I heard it go off. A few seconds later the starry signal displays itself beneath us.

Cold shivers run down my spine. If I had pulled the pistol up, it would have gone off in the machine, and we should have been roast meat before we reached the ground. In the darkness I did not notice that my mechanic had not merely loaded the pistol, but by mistake had cocked it as well.

The main thing, however, is that the pistol has fired its message. Its stars will tell the gunners below: "Germans!"

But their zeal makes them blind to the signal,

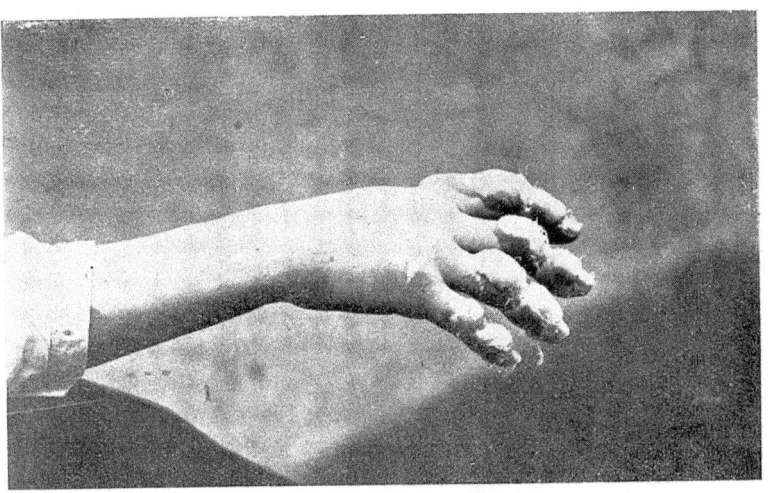

9     A FROST-BITTEN HAND

12     GERMAN AERODROME AT ATTIGNY

*Facing page 126*

or perhaps they take it for a trick of the enemy. Be that as it may, they send a new consignment of shells and shrapnels in our direction.

We are in a tight corner. Probably our people have not told Archie that we are still in the air, and so we must pay the bill of damages for their mistake. Let us hope that it will not be too high.

As we are flying at a height of 600 metres, we are on the horns of a dilemma. Our only way of escape from the shells is up into the thick clouds over our heads. But we do not want to go there; we are not particularly fond of clouds in the daytime, but at night, oh Lord! not at any price! And the few drops of benzine that remain to us will not suffice for a long detour.

Every now and then I shoot off a star-signal. Love's labour lost—they only go on potting at us!

Well, we might manage to stick it, but now they've got a search-light on the job. A search-light, heavens above!

Zuck! there comes the first beam of light. And zuck! there's another coming up on the left. My heart begins to thump. We are not so high now—quite low enough to be within reach of those rays of light, and our only means of informing the folk below that we are friends are our star-signals that they refuse to believe. Oh, how I'd like to hammer some sense into them with my fists!

How right is the old proverb: " I can defend myself against my enemies, but God preserve me from my friends! "

What a terrible prospect! To be dazzled by the searchlights of our own comrades and shot down after slinking so often past the French searchlights, worming our way through the French Archies, and scuttling for home with the French single-seaters on our trail!

Screwing up my eyes, I squint down at the searchlight on my right. A sly fellow—he hides his ray in one of the low-lying clouds and swings it round on to us when he catches the drone of our engine. The broad beam of light cuts a path through the air beneath us.

He simply must not catch us!

When I look round to see what the other searchlight is doing, in spite of my devilish fix I can't help laughing. On the farther side of the trenches, somewhere about the neighbourhood of the French aerodrome at Suippes, they are burning red magnesium flares. The French have spotted that the German Archies and searchlights are after us; consequently they take us for a *camarade* of the neighbouring army corps who has lost his way. They are now sending up a heap of red rockets to tell us: " Here you are! Come across this way! We're friends here! " I decline the kind invitation with thanks, despite the fact that my fellow-countrymen are behaving most hoggishly to me.

That searchlight is watching out for us again. Now he springs from his ambush, and this time he catches us. We are completely dazzled; the clouds of heaven and the lights of earth vanish from our eyes. The air all round us is glowing hot, and the light hurts our eyeballs as intensely as a couple of motor headlights at close quarters.

I want to shout to Take: "Go down," but it is superfluous. Instinctively he ducks his body forward so as to save his eyes from the dazzle of the terrible light, and his movement pushes the stick over so that we descend in a steep nosedive and escape into the darkness. The next moment Engmann evens out. (See sketch at chapter heading.)

"Switch off your engine!"

Now that the man at the searchlight can no longer hear the drone of our engine, he is uncertain of our whereabouts. Gleefully I watch his beam meandering through space like a will o' the wisp. Sometimes he comes quite near to us; then he wanders off in the opposite direction. We become quite cheerful again.

Engmann has to open out again to prevent us dropping lower. As soon as the two searchlight men hear our engine start, they begin to look for us again, and once more the spectral ray flashes alongside of us. Dazzled, I shut my aching eyes. But the light came and went too quickly for them to recognize us, and now we are getting beyond its radius.

I breathe freely once more and endeavour to take my bearings. I see familiar territory; we are over Vouziers, the Headquarters of our army.

And then I have to laugh again. All of a sudden the brightly lit town is plunged into darkness. The central has switched off the electric light.

"Enemy aircraft!"

I hastily fire my last star to ease their minds. To-morrow, of course, I shall be ticked off by Headquarters for disturbing their nightly peace and quiet. I'm sorry about the business—sorry for myself too.

Now we have only twelve more kilometres to Attigny. From our aerodrome a fog-bomb rises to tell me: "Here we are," and the red and green lights look almost near enough for me to touch them. If our benzine holds out, we'll do it. What a pity I cannot signal my safe homecoming to the good folk there!

And now they will surely hear the drone of our engine. But how are they to know who we are? If they suspect a bomb-throwing Frenchman they will put out the landing lights, and we shall have to come down on pitch-dark ground. I hope to goodness Engmann won't crash the machine!

In fact our people are bound to take us for the enemy because the lights in Vouziers went out, because someone there was certain to have got on the 'phone to them, because German searchlights dazzled us and German Archie potted at us, and now—oh, my word! they'll put out the lights in Attigny!

But somehow, despite all indications to the contrary, our friends down there sense that we are all right and leave the landing lights on.

When we are over the roofs of the darkened little town, Engmann throttles down his engine and lets the machine glide towards the coloured lights of the aerodrome. On our right the tall poplars rise up to meet us. We must open out again for a moment because we are not quite far enough on —then we glide again!

But now we are between the red lights—two rockets shoot up into the air to illumine the ground for us—aided by their light, Engmann makes a clean landing—we taxi on—our tail just touches the ground—ten, twenty metres we taxi—then we come to a stop.

Home once more!

Take stands up in his narrow cubby-hole and taps the emergency tank. It gives a hollow answer; it is almost empty.

"Not a farthing's worth of juice left," he tells me.

Through the struts between the centre section I dig him in the ribs. "A topping landing, Take, simply topping!"

While we wait for the crew of mechanics who have been racing alongside our wing tips as we taxied, other figures loom up out of the night. As the rockets have fizzled out, I only recognize them when they reach us. Captain Mohr is one of them.

"Thank Heavens you're back again safe and sound! We'd given you up. Come along to the mess, and we'll have a spot to wash out all the worry."

He beams as he hooks his arm in mine to drag me along to his car. But now it is my cue to put on the brakes.

"One minute, captain. I must see to my bombs first."

An icy silence. Some little time elapses before Captain Mohr recovers his power of speech.

"What? Your bombs? You brought your bombs back? You landed on our aerodrome with your bombs in this pitch-black, dark-as-sin night? Man alive, are you quite dotty?"

I feel somewhat aggrieved that the care I have taken of my precious bombs is rewarded in this shabby fashion.

"I got above the clouds," I tell him, "and could not find a target for them."

A ringing burst of laughter is his reply.

"Then chuck your eggs out anywhere you like, but don't bring them back to blow us all up. Do you think we'd have risked our precious lives if we'd guessed you'd got your damned bombs on board?"

Once more I try to justify myself, but Mohr interrupts me curtly.

"Shut your mouth, lieutenant! I'll tell you one thing, though," he relents, "your flight over the enemy and the finish of it over your hostile friends was A.1—no doubt about that. You're a hell of a fine airman, but, looking at the business from a military point of view, it was just too putrid for words. And now come on to the mess, and let us all have a chance of rubbing noses with the prodigal son!"

# CHAPTER XI

### ANXIOUS MOMENTS

AS we are about to cross the trenches by Aubérive-sur-Suippes at 3,300 we see shell-bursts from the Archies over Vaudesincourt, i.e., over German territory.

I decide to make for them.

With eyes alert, Engmann and I peer ahead. And, lo and behold! there's a Caudron fluttering about behind our lines!

"At her!"

Take stares questioningly at me through his goggles:

"What about our bombs?"

I wave my hand derisively. "Who knows whether the blighter will shoot back at us? And if he does, the odds are against him hitting the bombs. So we'll have a go at him!"

His conscience eased, Engmann nods his assent and chases after the Frenchman. As we are above him, we can go into a dive, by which we shall gain on him, although his is the faster machine on the level.

Meanwhile I search the air around, above and below us. A Frenchman doing reconnaissance work generally has two or three friends there to look after him. But to-day the enemy two-seater seems to be quite alone.

Then I turn to Engmann, who sits with bent back as he sights the enemy. Although we are still a good 400 metres away, the excited Take suddenly presses the trigger-button of his machine gun and rattles away. (See sketch at chapter heading.)

I am furious that he has let himself be carried away by his love of the chase and opened fire at such a distance. As the enemy had not yet seen us, we could have crept up to within 100 metres and pumped lead into him at close range.

Tack—tack—tack—tack——!

Four shots—then a jam! Bad luck! A few seconds later the Caudron has turned its nose to the front. Engmann follows him into a turn and attends to his machine gun. Once more he opens fire.

Tacktacktacktacktack!

Another jam! Simply heartbreaking! The very first time we had the luck to catch a lone flyer behind our lines this must happen. And to-day of all days, when we have tracer bullets in every fourth slot. The cartridges of this E ammunition are provided with smoke charges in their hinder parts which are ignited by the gases set up by the powder and leave a white trail of smoke behind them in the air, thus pointing out the right spot to put in a burst.

It's damnable! Now the Frenchman goes into a reckless nose dive to escape us. Engmann follows and opens fire for the third time, but after a few shots he is stopped by another jam.

Thanks to its superior speed the Caudron draws away from us. As it gains continually, it is useless for us to go on pursuing. So I whack Engmann, whose blood is up, into a right-hand turn which takes us back over the front.

. . . . .

After our failure it seems to me advisable to choose some other lines of approach to the enemy's territory. We have stirred up a wasps'-nest here in all likelihood, and if we go on, we are bound to get stung.

Accordingly I signal to our pugnacious Take to make a wide sweep in the hinterland behind our front and then steer for the Argonne. Ultimately we sneak across the front at Vienne-le-Château at a height of 4,000 in bright sunshine, with no cover from haze or clouds. Here we get another surprise, for now we are far beyond the French reserve positions and yet we have not seen a sign of a single shell or shrapnel, although Archies in this part of the world are as thick as blackberries. Something wrong about that! Experience has taught me that when I am flying over enemy territory, I must look for a snag in any untoward occurrence even though it seems to favour us. *Quidquid id est, timeo Danaos, et dona ferentes!* I do not trust our foe when he wears a benevolent aspect, and in nine cases out of ten my misgivings are well founded.

When I take a look round, I discover the cause of the silence. Dead under us, 2,000 metres below us, three Caudrons are circling round; probably they are spotting for the artillery. The lusty chorus of their six engines has drowned the weak solo of our one, so that the French Archies fail to hear us. I increase my glee at this let-off by sharing it with my good Take.

Over Ste Ménehould we get another surprise, which is not quite so pleasant. The Archie there are firing a new kind of shell; it bursts quite normally, but then some incendiary body emerges from its cloudlet and drops earthward in a curve, leaving a thick trail of smoke behind it.

I take the precaution of whacking Engmann off to Dampierre so that I can study this latest invention at a safe distance. Look before you leap! Probably the contraption is an incendiary shell of sorts, and what to our distant eyes looks like a thick column of smoke might turn out on nearer approach to be a veritable shower of burning phosphorus.

Ergo: keep our distance.

With these two incidents our daily list of surprises seems to be closed. The Châlons Archie, however, make it hot for us with several well-aimed shells that burst uncomfortably near.

The result of my observations is meagre: a couple of trains and some sort of a column on the road.

. . . .

I signal Take to throttle down.

"We'll bomb St. Hilaire station!" He nods and heads southward so as to approach the objective against the wind.

I have given several possible targets a miss. There is not much rolling-stock about at the stations to-day—and I must have a target that is worth while, because I mean to photograph the results. My camera is ready; I have only to press the release and do the trick.

I therefore make a careful examination of the bomb-rack. All safety catches have been released, and I have nothing to do but pull the lever.

Archie's first efforts, a series of dazzling white shrapnel cloudlets, are not particularly impressive. They are about 1500 metres too low and 2,000 too short.

A look round: in front, behind, right, left, above, below—not a sign of any hostile aircraft.

So now I study my objective again. We are a bit too much to the right. I give Engmann a gentle tap on the left shoulder, and he puts us into a gentle, cautious left turn. Yes, that's about right. I whack him between the shoulders, and he puts the machine into a straight course once more.

"Whoof!"

I look round in surprise. Close below us, to the left, I see a shell burst. Doesn't worry me now; we'll carry on. I confirm my resolution by whacking Engmann on the back to signify:

' Keep on straight ahead!"

A minute later the right moment comes. The grey sheds down there, near the rails, are a promising mark; they are full of war material, entrenching tools, straw, provisions and munitions.

"Whoof! whoof! whoof! whoof!"

To the left, above us, to the right, behind us— the air is full of shell cloudlets. And now a couple of shrapnels howl up at us: "Fee-ee-ee-ee-ee!"

We are in the middle of a spider's web of iron and lead. The wonted "what about it?" flashes into my brain and sets my heart beating. But I must not yield, now that I am so near my objective. While my ears register with increasing discomfort the detonations that come ever nearer, my eyes are sighting the railway lines through the spy-hole in the floor. As we are flying a straight course instead of approaching our target in a turn, it is not to be wondered at that Archie have taken so little time to get our range.

After a long, long minute the sheds make their appearance in my square spy-hole. I breathe a

## ANXIOUS MOMENTS

sigh of relief; good old Take has put in some masterful flying, and I simply can't miss. Now's the moment!

"Rrruck!"

Half a second later I send the other one down; almost at the same moment I bestow a jovial whack on Engmann's right shoulder and make signs to him with my hand in the mirror: "Home again!"

Whoof! Whoof!

Shells—a right and left—both about our exact height.

I whack Engmann's crash-helmet: "Dive!"

"Hah-ee-ee-ee!" yell the bracing wires.

As we dive down, the shells in the air seem to fly upward. A most agreeable sensation!

Well, Archie has done his worst now, and I can photograph the results of my bombing in comparative peace. With the camera in my hands I look down for them.

Now? now?

Aren't they ever going to burst? Perhaps they have both fallen in the sheds, so that I shall not see any smoke for a second or two. Putting the camera aside, I take a look through my glasses. The rails, trucks and buildings appear close enough to touch, but I can see no signs of any explosion.

Whoof!

A shell bursts just before our nose. Ah-ha! that's the front Archie trying to put up a barrage.

Engmann has put the machine into such a sharply-banked right-hand turn that I have to hang on to the pivot of my machine gun. We fly a half circle so that the next shells burst a good way behind us, and then we wriggle out of the worst of the fire in a series of irregular zigzags. Once again I search the station with my glasses. Nothing to be seen!

A scurvy reward for our dare-devil flight to the target and my careful aim under heavy fire! A dud, perhaps? Impossible; I've never had one yet! And now why should I suddenly get two? But why the devil can't I find any sign of the bursts?

Peevishly I cover up again the unexposed plate on which I had hoped to record two direct hits. Well, better luck next time!

A couple of ambitious shells try to catch us, but burst about a kilometre behind us.

As the altimeter indicates 1,700, I let Engmann cut his engine. "Such bad luck, Take," I inform him, "I couldn't get a snap of the bursts. And I was bang on the mark!"

He shrugs his shoulders in sympathy. A great pity we could not manage it!

When I pull down the railway map to glance over my entries, I see something that makes my blood run cold—the two bombs! I take a close look at them. It was entirely my own fault, because I sent the second one down too quickly after the first. Consequently the fat part of bomb No. 2 jammed the stabilizing ring of bomb No. 1 in the narrow hole. Both were wedged, and neither left the machine.

## ANXIOUS MOMENTS

At the same moment Engmann cuts his engine again.

"Main tank empty," he yells at me. "I must switch on to the emergency!"

I bend over to him. "We must get back over the front again, Take. The two bombs are jammed. We can't land with them because they may go off any moment!"

There is an expression of dismay on Engmann's face as he turns cautiously towards the front. Laboriously we fight our way back against the strong south wind.

I bend down in the cockpit to investigate the situation, and the shock I get makes my heart stand still. Those bombs have slipped down a bit. The hard knocks they will get from the vibrations of the engine that set everything in the machine a-quiver will cause them to slide ever deeper until finally their weight will force the thin wood of the trap to open. Then they will fall on German territory, in the middle of a German column, or in a German camp in the woods perhaps—and kill ever so many of our German brethren——

The situation does not bear thinking about. And I cannot possibly wait until we are on the French side of the line again. But I shall have to, if I can. Yes, I must get hold of the handle of the lower bomb somehow and hold tight on to it until we have flown over the front once more.

I bend down into the cockpit, but cannot get my head into a position to look down into the bomb-hole because of my helmet. I tear it off and my goggles as well. Ah, that's better. I feel my way down the hole with a cautious arm. No, I can't get hold of it! Simply maddening! Every moment those devilish things are slipping deeper and deeper. And now I realize another danger, for I can see that the wind of our aeroplane's propeller is making the little propellers on the bombs revolve. They are supposed to revolve in the air until the firing pin is opposite the detonator, but they are revolving now; the safety device is released, in all probability. They only need a strong shake to burst and blow us to pieces in mid air!

Necessity is the mother of invention. I take a couple of pencils and thrust them cautiously between the blades of the little propellers so as to stop them revolving.

And now, how am I to get hold of the handles and stop those bombs going down on to German territory? If only I had a bit of wire or cord! I look round in quest of something. An isolation band? No, too weak! Wait a moment—there's the very thing—my scarf!

Hastily I loosen it from my neck and cautiously push its end towards the handle of the lower bomb with my screwdriver. After several fruitless efforts I contrive to pass it through, pull it up again, grab the two ends of the scarf in my left fist and raise myself carefully from the floor.

The worst danger is over. With a sigh of relief I wipe the sweat from my brow—yes, I was perspiring when the temperature was two degrees below zero! I look overboard. Ah, we are just passing our reserve positions at Moronvilliers. Slowly we push our way past the German trenches and then past the French ones. I have no time to bother about the shells and shrapnels that are howling all around us.

Now we are flying over the French reserve positions, and a few minutes later a woodland camp comes into view. That's the place for my two bombs! I cautiously extract my scarf again; then, with my right hand, I pull up the handle of the uppermost bomb. The lower one is released from its jam, and, whizz! down it goes!

A load passes from my mind, but the next moment I swear irritably. I have forgotten to remove the pencil I jammed between the bomb's propeller blades. Now my chance has gone; as the propeller will not revolve, the firing-pin will not act on the detonator. Is that what you call rising to the situation, Herr Heydemarck? The finder of that dud bomb will be most surprised when he discovers the pencil.

As these bright but belated thoughts have occupied my brain for the merest fraction of a second, I have at least time to remove the pencil from bomb No. 2. Then I despatch it on its way.

Thank Heaven, I am now rid of those devilish eggs! Unfortunately I have neither time nor opportunity to watch what happens to them, for, as we have steered a straight course, the Archie have got our range so accurately that we must make tracks at once. With the help of a couple of whacks on the head good old Take does the needful. Then the strong south wind catches us and whirls us along. Our benzine is good for only another ten minutes, but with such a breeze at our backs we shall easily make Attigny.

And—we have got away with it again!

## CHAPTER XII

#### NIGHT SWARMS

IN July, the month of the war harvest, our ranks were sadly thinned. Fifty per cent of our little group of twelve were gone : two dead, one severely and three lightly wounded.

To make good our losses Captain Mohr had a brainwave that prompted him to send us out on " reconnaissances in force," which were to be carried out by chains of three Machines. Although we could manage our jobs much better on our lonesomes, friend Max Mohr was not to be reasoned out of his idea, and so we had to do as we were told.

I had to lead the first chain, and thought I looked rather a funny object with the long streamers floating from my wing-tips. (See sketch at chapter-heading.)

As we had our hands and eyes full up on the way with observations, photography and bombing, and so were unable to watch one another's movements, we lost each other on the outward trip " by mistake on purpose " and met again, as I had carefully arranged with Holzhausen and Beckmann, over Bazancourt at a height of 2,000 metres on the way back. Thence we flew back proudly to Attigny in wedge formation and landed after flying a circle round the aerodrome to show ourselves off. A pious fraud, which was followed by a pious lie. Luckily the chief showed himself accessible to our united requests, and consequently this deceptive manœuvre was our last as well as our first " reconnaissance in force."

. .

One night in the mess we were chatting about the squadron flight to Revigny, which was more or less of a wash-out and always a fruitful topic for mirth. Suddenly Captain Mohr put a damper on our high spirits.

" He who laughs last, laughs best, gentlemen. The next cloudless night all aircraft attached to the 3rd Army Corps will be sent out." But when he saw our dismay, his features relaxed into a jovial grin. " Don't look as if you'd seen the devil, boys," he assured us, " I was only pulling your legs. This time we are going to throw over our dear old official principle of : ' Why do things in a simple way when there's a complicated way for them ? ', and instead of the squadron flight you'll be called upon to do a swarm flight. Orders: bombs to be dropped on all the quarters of the enemy's staff. Two machines of our little lot will bomb the Headquarters at Châlons, while the other two will make things hum at La Cheppe."

I laughed. " Our G.H.Q. is feeling bold," I suggested, " and what will the consequences be? What saith the old adage? If you beat my Jew, I shall beat yours. Whereupon it follows: If the German airman takes pot shots at the French generals, then the French airmen will have to have a smack at the German generals." As, indeed, it came to pass later.

A fine, starry night.

Engmann twists himself round in the pilot's seat as far as his safety-belt will allow him.

" Ready? " he asks.

" Ready! "

" Look out! " he screams to the two members of the starting squad that stand to right and left of our wings. Then the rustle of the engine swells to a mighty roar, and we roll up to the starting-point. When the impetuous propeller of our great bird tries to push us along too quickly, Engmann throttles down a peg or two to put a damper on its exuberance.

I bend forward and stare over into the weakly illuminated pilot's compartment. What's the time? 3.10 a.m., says the little clock. Another five minutes before we're due off, then. We roll slowly up to the end of the field, where a red magnesium flare gleams beside the big wood fire. Our other three birds flit about like fantastic ghosts.

With the light of my pocket-torch I take a look round the interior of my own domain. Everything O.K. The four twelve-and-a-half kilo bombs that are destined for La Cheppe to-night rest peacefully in their rack.

One minute more! I feel for the ends of my broad safety-belt and buckle myself in. You never know what may happen on these nightly starts . . .

Our engine is slow to fire and misses 400 revs., meanwhile spitting huge sparks from the exhaust.

3.15 a.m.

" Off ! " shouts the squadron leader to us and raises his arm. The engine fires—we open out three pegs—now full on—we taxi—faster and faster—our tail rises from the ground—a bit of a hop—and we are soaring in the air.

I whack Engmann into a straight course for the front. With the south wind against us we shall climb to 2,000 before we pass the trenches—and, besides, it's night.

I turn my torch on to the altimeter : 200.

I glance round and look for the aerodrome. The red flare makes it easy to find. And, hallo ! there's the last of our machines just starting. I can see it as a tiny point of light as it taxies.

No moonlight, only starlight. Amazing to find

the visibility so good below us. Under our feet lies Attigny ; I recognize the town by the street-lamps and a few illuminated windows. To eastward lies the station—a pearl necklace of arc lamps.

We feel our way along the high road and then steer a southward course. No sign of the trenches as yet, but the distant rockets and starshells give us an indication of its position. Every now and then the blackness of night is torn by lurid flashes : the artillery is at work. Farther eastward, where we are in the midst of an offensive against Verdun, flashes burst out uninterruptedly at a hundred—no, a thousand points. Drum fire. But we hear nothing, for the roar of our engine drowns all other noises.

The altimeter shows 1,200. We have flown over Somme Py and are approaching the trenches. I can spy the gleams of light from the reserve positions, while the next rocket that goes up gives me a glimpse of the front line. The lurid magnesium light reveals in surprisingly sharp outlines all the shellholes and mounds of debris in the scarred, chalky soil.

The French have heard the drone of our engine and endeavour to spot us with their rockets. A quick series of these luminaries shoots up towards us. We see a big flash below us—something invisible flies up to us—a long comet's tail expands—its hundred thousand sparks dance in the air—some object that gleams dully leaps from the invisible body behind the burning tail and bursts with a hurried crack—and glides slowly earthwards in the bright light. Sustained in the air by its little silk parachute, it takes a full minute to reach the ground. Do the French really think they are going to spot us with those silly fireworks?

Now we have left the region of the scarred chalkland far behind us. Look—a flash; from Suippes arises a broad beam that bores its way through space towards us. A searchlight!

Brrrr!

After our unhappy nightly adventure with our German friends, we have taken a dislike to searchlights, no matter what their nationality may be. They awaken unpleasant memories in our minds —gleaming light, strong as sunlight in our eyes— inability to see anything—eyes dazzled—machine crashes!

That is the doom that now threatens us! I whack Engmann into a series of zigzags so as to make it difficult for that damned *éclair* down below to spot us. The man who works it cannot see us; he can only hear us and must therefore fumble for the drone of our engine.

Zuck! zuck! zuck-zuck! it shoots through the sky like an arrow; now it is above us, now below us. Once the beam streaks along at our side, and I have to shut my aching eyes. But its pace was too quick, and now it is busily searching the realm of space beyond us.

I signal Engmann to throttle down so as to muffle the sound that gives our direction to those fellows below. The ruse succeeds; the beam flickers restlessly hither and thither. But several minutes later we have to open up our engine in order to keep from dropping too low.

Promptly the antenna of light fumbles its way towards us. But we are now well beyond its most effective range, so that its ray is too weak to harm us. We continue to fly a straight southward course.

Ten minutes later we espy a narrower band that emerges from the high road which is our guide and bears sharply to the left. That is the old Roman road, and over there, where it intersects the dark-meadowed valley, is La Cheppe.

Hallo! there's another searchlight! But it comes from somewhere near Bussy-le-Château—more than three kilometres away. But even if it were located at La Cheppe itself, it is not going to stop us now. With gentle taps on the shoulder I direct Engmann towards the village.

That's it—straight ahead now. The searchlight flits uneasily to and fro; when I signal Take to throttle down for half a minute, the men who direct its beam lose their heads and send it zigzagging crazily all over the sky. They get nowhere near us until our engine is going once more—and then it is too late.

At intervals of one second I drop my four bombs.

Then Engmann gets a hard whack on his left shoulder: "left-hand turn!" This manœuvre brings us broadside on to the searchlight so that its beam can only catch our flank. It therefore cannot dazzle our eyes.

I bend overboard to observe the effect of my

bombs. As we are now flying over the dark terrain of the valley, I can make out the village street and the outlines of the farmhouses.

And then I see flashes on the ground—bomb No. 1 too short! No. 2 on the edge of the village! No. 3 farther in! No. 4 bang in the middle!

Satisfied with our work, we fly off back to the front. This time we know where those searchlights are located. We fly round them in respectful curves and rejoice to find that the beams which have travelled such a long way through the darkness and haze are so pale when they reach us that they cannot dazzle our eyes. I stare at them boldly and note their locations on my map; perhaps some day one of us can spoil their beauty with a bomb.

 . . . . .

As we flew to our objective by the shortest way and returned home again immediately, we made a good landing in Attigny exactly an hour and a quarter after we had taken off.

Quite an easy business—this swarm flight! Everyone for himself, and no one to mess up my job!

But I found I was wrong in this impression. A few minutes after our arrival, No. 2, the other La Cheppe machine, landed, and half an hour later came No. 3, one of the couple that had visited Châlons.

Time passed on and we still waited for the return of No. 4, who had also dropped his eggs on the G.H.Q. But our ears could not catch the drone of his engine. Missing! though there's still a chance he may have landed at some other German aerodrome Just as we were about to return to the town with heavy hearts, Captain Mohr was called to the telephone. He came back laughing. " No need to worry, gentlemen ! The truant has made a happy landing. He got to Châlons all right, but lost his way coming home and overshot the mark by thirty-five kilometres. Apparently he is a zealous student of military history, for he's made a trip to Sedan."

Relieved, we joined in his laugh.

. . . . .

Not long afterwards our scouts shot down a French single-seater, and we asked the lieutenant who was its pilot about the success of our night swarm.

" Oh, the smartest of them all was the fellow who bombarded La Cheppe," he replied.

My heart swelled with pride. Holzhausen had bombed the same objective, but, of course, the good shot was mine.

" By an unhappy chance he hit the hospital," continued the Frenchman.

My heart shrunk to something mean and ugly. Why should it be my bomb that hit the hospital? I was certain that it must have been Holzhausen's.

" Luckily there was no loss of life. The bomb fell right on the red cross made of bricks that we put in the courtyard."

My heart resumed its normal proportions. As far as I was concerned, it might remain uncertain whether the bomb was Holzhausen's or mine !

## CHAPTER XIII

#### BOMBING EPERNAY STATION

ABOUT 4 a.m. I issued the bombs for the dawn patrol. Shortly after 6 a.m. Holzhausen rang me up from the aerodrome.

"Sorry, but I must ask you to come along because I couldn't get rid of my bombs."

When I arrived, he recounted me his experiences.

"Air simply thick with enemy to-day! When we crossed the lines over Aubérive, two Nieuports made for us. We were potting at each other for quite a long time. They hung on to me like leeches, so that I had no chance of reconnoitring. I had to sound the retreat."

"And I suppose you tried to get through somewhere else "

Holzhausen laughed. " Well, yes, we did—over Rheims. We got a bit further into enemy territory. Then we had two more of them after our scalps—a Nieuport and a Caudron this time. They were working the new tactics, of course, one diving on to us from above, while the other came up at us from below. The result was naturally the same as with our first effort—simply impossible to think of reconnoitring while they hung on to us."

" And in spite of them you didn't get rid of your bombs ? "

He shook his head vigorously. " Lord, no, the bally things cost too much money ! But you'd better hear the rest of my tale ! Naturally I had a third shot at getting through. We took the precaution of flying back ten kilometres our side of the line, and then we crossed it at Massiges. The result ? Well, they had us taped as soon as we were over the French reserve positions, with this difference : there weren't merely two of them but half a dozen. As we were running short of benzine, I felt I'd had enough and beat it. So here I am again, and I can't help it."

I scratched my head thoughtfully. " I'm on the second patrol to-day," I said, " and I'm supposed to cross the front at 3 p.m. sharp because we want to get an idea of the enemy's railway traffic at that time. So I shall arrive just when aerial activity is at its height. If the French machines are so busy in the morning, I'm in for a lovely time after lunch."

Holzhausen nodded sympathetically.

"I can only wish you a good digestion," he said.

.   .

Before we start I show Engmann the new wind report.

"Capital!" I declare. "Firstly, there's a tough east wind of ninety kilometres an hour velocity at 4,000 metres, so naturally we'll cross the line by the Argonne and get it to shove us along. Secondly, there are strong gusts all the way up to the ceiling, which will mean there won't be so much doing in the air as there was this morning."

We whirl off with two twenty-kilo bombs on board.

The gusts are no laughing matter. They shake us up so much that I buckle myself in so as not to be thrown out in an unguarded moment. That done, I entrust myself blindly to Engmann's air sense.

A pleasant surprise awaits us when we fly over the front. From the Meuse friendly clouds roll up; the wind, it is true, has torn them to shreds, but "every little helps."

Now we are over the German positions. When a few scraps of cloud come sailing along, we rise quickly above them and rejoice in the cover they afford us. But our joy is of no long duration, for this blanket is torn away from under our feet while we are still over the German trenches. We have no better luck when we try to hide ourselves in another wreath of clouds floating somewhat higher; moreover, we encounter violent gusts that set all our machine's joints creaking when we enter and when we leave their shelter. I therefore decline all further offers of such cover with polite thanks and decide to cross the enemy's lines in the bright sunshine.

And now we have passed over a large part of the French Archie's field of range without getting a single shot. Nevertheless, Engmann makes assurance doubly sure by letting the east wind drift him sideways and putting the machine into a series of irregular zigzags.

Hallo! Whoof! whoof! half left before us burst two shells of a poisonous yellow hue. Our eyes tell us that they are exceedingly well aimed—the clouds of their smoke appear as large as life. Our ears confirm the unpleasant tidings, because we cannot help hearing their detonations in spite of the hellish roar of our engine. Very mean of the enemy to be potting at us from this neighbourhood where there never used to be any Archie. Well, let's hope it's not a permanent battery, but just one of those lorry affairs that will clear off again. (See sketch at chapter heading.)

But our surprises are by no means finished. After sending up those two shells the gunners below cease fire. Expectantly I scan the ground to ascertain the battery's next movement. The tension becomes intolerable, but minutes pass by as we fly on.

Then at last it dawns on me that those two

shells are all we are going to get. I shrug my shoulders uncomprehendingly. This is something new in my experience; those shells had our range beautifully, and yet the gunners are not going to follow them up with others. Still, we have no objection to pleasant surprises of that sort.

When I think the matter over, a possible explanation occurs to me. Perhaps there is a French aeroplane somewhere about in our neighbourhood. I hastily peer overboard and search the air . . . far and wide, not a tail to be seen. I cannot even see any aeroplanes in front of the hangars belonging to the two Ste Ménehould aerodromes.

And why were the bursts such a poisonous yellow hue? " Yellow with rage " is Take's explanation, but I cannot accept it.

Meanwhile we have reached Ste Ménehould, where the outburst of fire from the local Archie puts an end to my meditations. When I have whacked Engmann into a north-west course, we get the forceful east wind behind us; its ninety kilometres an hour are added to our own 126. This fact gives me such pleasure that I have to let Engmann share it, and he shows his delight with his usual " polar bear " wagging of the head. But the next moment he has to put the brake on his oscillations to dodge a gust. We don't usually meet such boisterous fellows at a height of 4,000 metres.

The hangars and tents of most of the other aerodromes seem to be closed. At Suippes I can

# BOMBING EPERNAY STATION

see two Caudrons and a Nieuport on the ground; otherwise, everything's as quiet as a cemetery. We therefore make a detour to include Châlons in our itinerary, from which town we proceed along the banks of the Marne. Observation possibilities are good to-day, and my eleven photos will develop well.

So now we have only to get rid of our bombs. As the target is left to my discretion, I decide to unload them on Ay station, a place that has never been favoured with our attentions. I therefore whack Engmann into a turn so that we can approach our objective against the wind. But I forget the powerful driving force of that east wind, which pushes us across the Marne towards the adjacent Epernay before we can circle round.

I cannot help laughing. Very well, we'll try our luck here. It is all to our advantage that we can fly down the long side of the station premises against the east wind. With a second's interval between them, my two bombs whirl earthwards.

I have managed it beautifully. One bomb hits a big shed while the other falls on the lines between two rows of trucks. A mighty cloud of smoke hangs over the station; it is not merely the mixture of the bomb's gases with the earth and debris the explosion has thrown up—no, I have hit a consignment of munitions and blown it up sky high!

Quick, quick! My camera! It lies ready to my hand. One moment, though, I must change the plate first. I pull the plateholder out by its tag and push another in. Oh, Lord! plate broken! jammed . . . can't get it out again . . . oh, what brutal luck!

When I have whacked Engmann into a northerly course towards the front, I show him the smoking station as he goes into the turn, so that he can share my pleasure.

.   .

When Take showed me the barogram of our flight, we understood why we had encountered no hostile aircraft. The normal perfection of its curves (see page 56) was sadly marred by the violent gusts, which had caused the needle to squirt several blobs of ink on to the paper.

.   .   .   .

We were all very sorry that I had been unable to secure a photo of my two good shots. Several days later, however, my heart was gladdened by the confirmation I received from a notice in the press.

"AIR RAID ON EPERNAY.

"Paris, May 2nd. According to the *Temps*, a German aeroplane flew over Epernay last Saturday afternoon and dropped two bombs which caused considerable damage.

## CHAPTER XIV

### INTO THE MIST

I WAS standing with Engmann beside our machine, which was ready to start. "Well, Take, what do you think of the weather?" I inquired.

He raised his nose to sniff the early morning air.

"I don't trust it. The air is damp and warm together—that means a ground-mist as soon as the sun's up. We'd better wait a bit."

I shook my head.

"No, nothing doing, my lad. The weather is just right for a long-distance reconnaissance. If the ground-mist gets up, we'll just land at the first handy aerodrome on our way back. We'll chance it, and if the worst comes to the worst, we'll sneak through somehow."

Half an hour later we zoom up between Vouziers and Rethel and make for the front at a height of 2,500. But when I look round, a mild shiver runs through all my limbs—the ground-mist is creeping up!

Slowly the wind wafts an even bank of grey mist over the awakening earth. To north-westward—as far as my eye can reach—there is a grey shroud, the front edge of which is relieved by delicate mosaics, like those formed by the sand layers on the bed of a stream.

What about it? Either we must come down at once—or we must carry on with our reconnaissance, in which case we are bound to have an awful landing in the mist when we return.

But not for a moment am I in two minds about the business. Neither yesterday nor the day before could we make a reconnaissance; it is therefore absolutely necessary that I should utilize the present opportunity. The front and the country behind it that I must reconnoitre are still free of mist.

While the sun creeps over the bank of mist in the east as a dull, rayless disc, I signal Engmann to throttle his engine and shout in his ear:

" Front via Rheims! "

Our flight takes place under a lucky star. Although we have penetrated as far as Vertus and flown back by Châlons, we have not had a single fight in the air. I decide to mark this as a red-

## INTO THE MIST

letter day in my diary. Our reconnaissance, too, was satisfactory: only slight traffic at St. Hilaire junction, but considerable rolling stock on the stretch between Châlons and the front—four long troop trains, following one another at intervals of five kilometres.

When we have reached Ste Ménehould on our way back, Engmann points ahead and snaps his fingers. The ground mist has advanced far enough to swallow up the French trenches.

It is pleasant to think that we shall not be spotted and peppered by Archie, but there is a big snag ahead. How are we to find our own aerodrome again? Worse still: can we even make sure of landing behind the German lines?

I scan the air hastily for hostile aircraft, and it is well I do so. Two Caudrons are coming up on us from behind.

They are still a good kilometre away and several hundred metres below us. We should have had a nasty shock, all the same, if they had been able to fasten on to our tail unseen and put in a few bursts. The day which began so promisingly cannot be marked as a red-letter one after all.

But we have done our job, and are on the way home. So come on, you blighters! I warn Engmann in order to spare his nerves a shock when I suddenly rattle away, and then let the propeller wind swing our machine gun round. The game can begin!

As the pair of them are still well out of range, I have time to take a look ahead through our wings. We have to fly another five kilometres of open country before reaching the ground-mist, which is therefore not an urgent problem at the moment. First I must deal with those two——

"Tack-tack-tack-tack-tack..."

I turn round in horror. What is the meaning of that sudden burst? Three seconds ago I saw with my own eyes that those two Caudrons were at least 800 metres away! As my body swings round, I release the machine gun's safety-catch and sink on to one knee so as to shoot upward. At the same time I look up and see a Nieuport diving on to us. "All good things are three," says the proverb, but it is a good thing for us that No. 3 is not a tough customer. He has opened fire much too soon.

I spit out a short series of bullets in his direction, just to tell him: "I'm quite ready, *mon ami*." Meanwhile Engmann has not exactly been asleep, for he has gone into a sharp turn which takes us out of the burst—if we were ever in it. I have a brotherly affection for him when he reacts so quickly to these unforeseen incidents, which are, so to speak, a portion of our daily bread.

That cheeky blighter up there makes me laugh. He used those two Caudrons as decoys to spring his surprise on us. But my laugh is a shamefaced one, however, because I have let him make a fool of me.

Once again I send the Nieuport a short series of bullets. Then I wait—eyes skinned... finger on trigger-button. As the Nieuport is still shooting,

## INTO THE MIST

Engmann goes into another turn. Ah! now I've got him sighted again.

Tack-tack-tack-tack-tack!

When I pause, I get a pleasant surprise. To-day, for the first time, I have some of those new smoke bullets in my belt. They indicate the right spot for a burst by exploding in the air and leaving nice trails of smoke behind them.

There's the first of them. Looks very nice! Has the Nieuport spotted the trick? Apparently not, for he carries on undisturbed. I must give him another dose and let him have a good view of my novelties.

Tack-tack-tack-tack-tack . . .

Now there are three puffs of smoke in the air between him and us, and he can hardly overlook them. He sees them, and the surprise is such a painful one that he sheers off in a steeply-banked turn. I cease fire and nudge Engmann so that he can share my glee.

I turn back to deal with my three-leafed clover again. But meanwhile one leaf is sadly faded, for the Nieuport has taken his leave. The two Caudrons, however—as yet too far away to notice our novelty—are still approaching. They evidently do not intend to outclimb us, but will close on us from below like a pair of pincers.

I am curious to see if their reactions will resemble those of the Nieuport and can hardly await the moment when I may display my little puffs of smoke to them. Now they are within 400 metres . . . so come on!

Thirty shots—with four smokers—to the fellow on my right.

Tack—tack—tack—tack—tack . . .

Then a similar dose for his friend on my left.

Tack—tack—tack—tack—tack . . .

The results are decidedly pleasing, for both Caudrons sheer off. When they come out of their turns, they hang around, but take care to keep outside a respectful radius of 800 metres.

So now I have time for another look round. I find that we must have flown over the edge of the mist-field some time ago, for now we are above a sea of whiteness. The Caudrons appear to have reached similar conclusions, for they abandon all further pursuit and make off.

Good-bye, dear friends!

So now I can give all my attention to the solution of our final problem, which is to find our way back to Attigny.

From my compass I endeavour to ascertain the possible whereabouts of our aerodrome, and calculate that it must lie somewhere in the direction of the point marked by 348 degrees. Having whacked Engmann into the desired course, I look out to my right where the sunshine casts the sharply-outlined shadows of the struts across our wings. I quickly visualize the scene.

"Switch off!"

Engmann pulls his lever back and tilts his head over so as to catch my words.

"Fly so as to keep the shadows in the same positions. We may find a hole over Vouzier

## INTO THE MIST

through which we can worm our way. Drop a bit in case we can catch a glimpse of the ground."

Engmann nods and goes into a glide with his engine throttled down to half.

I reflect. From Ste Ménehould to the front we took ten minutes against the wind. According to my calculations another eighteen minutes should bring us somewhere near Vouziers at about 8.5 a.m.

For the moment I have nothing to do but take care that we hold our course above the mist. Meditatively I glance down at the white plain beneath me. Is it a ground-mist hugging the soil or has the sun shone long enough to suck it up and turn it into clouds? I strain my eyes downward to discover the correct solution, but from our 1,500 metres I cannot even make a guess at the approximate height of the mist's upper surface. Is it 100 metres? or 1,000? I cannot tell. Sometimes it looks as if our undercarriage must be scraping the white blanket, while at others I feel inclined to say to Engmann : "Drop a bit—go on dropping!" (See Illustration No. 13.)

A glance at our clock: 8.2 a.m. Then we must be getting near Vouziers. We have held a straight course, for the shadows of the struts lie at the same angle. The north-west wind may have drifted us over to the right a bit, but as our course is north-west, it can only be a trifle.

8.5 a.m. According to my calculation we ought to be over Vouziers by now. The altimeter points to 1,000, but we have not yet dropped to the level of the mist, and there are no signs of earth beneath us.

No alternative but to carry on along our old course.

8.10 a.m. Now we are diving into the cobwebby veil. We must take care not to sink too deep into this Nirvana. Better an hour of Archie than reel about in a mist and end with a crash.

From above the enfeebled light of the sun's pale disc still filters down to us; it is the only fixed point by which we can conserve our sense of equilibrium. Engmann keeps on casting quick looks to one or other side in the hope of seeing something that will enable him to keep the machine on an even keel.

If only no mountainous clouds tower over us as we fly onward and swallow the sun! That would be the last straw! I peer downward, but my straining eyes can see no sign of earth.

All at once the last shimmer of sunshine goes. I look at the compass; its glass is clouded over. Deeper and deeper we glide into the milky whiteness; darker and darker becomes the space around us.

That means that the mist has not yet lifted. The sun has not yet sucked it up to form a cloud. It is still hugging the earth. It would be madness to dive farther into the depths. We should run the risk of hitting the ground with a bang or ramming some obstacle such as a house, a hillock, a tree, or a telephone wire.

" Open your engine! " I shout to Engmann.

" Hi! " screams the propeller as it whirls round once more. But a dull tone creeps into the song of our engine that is usually so clear.

FLYING OVER GROUND MIST

## INTO THE MIST

Out of the ghastly hell! Up to the sun again!

But still the sun remains hidden. At last its pale disc gleams dully above us—now there are only a few films of cobwebs between us and its brightness—and now the last of them has vanished. From the underworld we have swung ourselves aloft to the light—oh, joy of joys! And the engine rejoices with us in the bright, clear song that it sings again. Hail, oh sun!

Our machine is dripping with moisture—just as if it had been pulled out of the sea. The drops form little streams which run down the sides of the cockpit and our leather jackets. Our great double-decker seems to shake itself like a sparrow after a bath in a puddle. We, too, shake ourselves, and wipe the water from our goggles.

What next? What direction——?

From the sun and my compass I observe that we have turned nearly 180 degrees in the mist. We are now flying back to the front; we are flying south-east instead of north-west.

I quickly make up my mind and signal Engmann to throttle down again.

"This is a hell of a mess, Take! Fly back to the front and climb. We are bound to find a spot where the fogbank is not so thick. We'll feel our way earthwards then and fly back to Attigny under the mist. Carry on!"

Engmann puts our bird into a climbing turn. Back to the front we go. Eagerly I look down, but nowhere can I spy the dark mass of the earth beneath me.

My imagination doubles the speed at which every minute passes by. Now we have the wind behind us—we are flying southwards—towards, towards the enemy.

Over there—at last—at last! Between two mountains of clouds I spy something dark. It is barely visible, but I hail it with joy.

When I have given the signal to glide on Engmann's helmet, I bend over and show him the dark patch.

"Down there!"

He nods: "Right ho!" and throttles down his engine.

1,500—1,200—1,000—800—600——

We descend in narrow spirals to the earth which still remains an unseen element. Anxiously we grope for our Mother Earth's hand, which will lead us out of all our tormenting anxieties.

Higher and higher tower the mountains of clouds above us with every metre that we drop. Now they are 200—300 metres above us. As from some deep cup in the hills I stare up the sides of those mighty, ever-darkening mountains to the patch of blue sky that diminishes every moment.

100——

Now I can distinguish the landscape, as though through a veil. Stretches of barren sand—copses—moors of heather—fields of brown grass, and yet it is Paradise to us because no white chalk gleams upward. That means that we are not near the trenches.

Now I can see well enough to feel my way along

## INTO THE MIST

the ground. A glance at my compass gives me the north.

Engmann has meanwhile opened out his engine, and I whack him into a wide right-hand turn which will put us in the direction of home. But suddenly he turns round to me.

"Back to the French?" he shouts.

I have to laugh heartily at his dismay.

"No, no. We're just about somewhere over La Neuville, I reckon. So carry on!"

He nods in satisfaction and opens out his engine again. I glance behind me. The little speck of blue sky that I could see just now has become greyer and greyer . . . at last it vanishes. The mist has swallowed us up—skin and bones and all. But what do we care? Now we have the earth—to which our senses can hold fast. Suddenly a white mass of chalk looms up out of the mist. It is a new railway cutting, from which the smoke of an engine curls up to add its little contribution to the excess of vapour in the air.

We feel our way along the railway lines until we reach a village.

Now I have my bearings again.

"Cauroy!" I shout to Engmann.

He nods and wriggles on his seat to show his delight. Now all is well with us! It is child's play to find our way home by the road!

Shortly afterwards he has to throttle down his engine for a few seconds because we have climbed a bit and penetrated the thick mass of the fog again. Then we circle respectfully around

Machault in case a sudden gust should crash us into the houses, and when the danger is past, we rejoin the main road once more. For us it is Ariadne's thread, to which we must hold fast.

Now the trees, which flank the road on either side, climb up over a hillock where the mist still clings to the ground. Several tense seconds pass —shall we clear this obstacle? Yes, we'll just do it! We hop over the hillock with a couple of metres to spare. Another village—that will be Lessincourt. In the yards I can see soldiers grooming horses. We can distinguish their white faces quite plainly when they look up to us. Once again Engmann has to throttle down because we are rising into the mist.

Along the broad road marches a company of infantry, headed by their captain on his cob. Whew! we have passed them already! (See sketch at chapter heading.)

While I am still looking back at them, Engmann suddenly throttles down his engine and shouts our war whoop.

" Hoy-ee-ee-ee-ee ! "

As I bend over to him in some amazement, he waves his left arm triumphantly. What is the joyful discovery that has whirled him into such excitement?

We are flying over the " Spider's Web," as we term the junction of the six cross-roads west of Vouziers. It is a landmark that we cannot possibly mistake.

While Engmann goes into another glide I yell

our war whoop so loudly that the good folk in the neighbouring farmyard stare up at us in astonishment. But before they can open their mouths, the mist has swallowed us up again.

All at once the road before us vanishes into a thick mass of dirt. That is the hillock that masks our aerodrome from the inquisitive eyes of the observers in the French captive balloons. Can we clear it? Engmann throttles down again, and we sink ever deeper and deeper.

"Bump!" A vigorous gust catches us under the right wing and tries to lever us up. "Ratch!" Engmann parries its blow by pushing the stick over.

Bravo, Take!

On the crest of the little hill there is a French trench that dates back to our advance in 1914. What if such times came again! After we have flown over the hillock, the mist gradually lifts from the earth. Soon afterwards the first houses of our beloved Attigny loom into sight. I fire a star-signal to warn the good folk at the aerodrome of our arrival. Besides, they will hear the drone of our engine.

We circle round the town in a respectful curve and then head for the aerodrome.

And now the hangars loom up. Near the landing-pylon a red flame quivers. Strange how the mist swallows its rays, so that only little red pin-points reach us! A short glide—our wheels touch the ground—our tail scrapes behind them—we have made a good landing.

Joyfully we scramble out of the cockpit. Ah, there is the squadron-leader whose anxiety on our behalf has driven him out to the aerodrome.

"Beg to report myself back from my flight, sir."

He shakes both our hands. "An acrobatic stunt!" he says.

His greeting is laconic enough, but we can feel that he shares our joy.

## CHAPTER XV

### CUCKOO !

AN hour before sunrise.
"Bombs safely on board?" I inquire.

Lance-Corporal Sievers sticks his head out of the cockpit for a moment.

"Ready in a couple of minutes."

"Good! Come along, Take, and I'll show you what I've planned for to-day."

We stumble over the lowered door into the lighted hangar and study our map at a mechanic's bench.

"Orders: Reconnoitre up to the Marne. But with a favourable wind behind us we can add on an extra bit and do a long-distance reconnaissance as far as Mailly, that place of happy memories. As the weather forecast prophesies south-westerly winds, we can cross the front at Rheims and push on southward as far as Fère-Champenoise. Then we turn eastward and drop our bombs on Vitry-le-François station."

When the starting squad have lit the beacon that will give us our direction, we start off.

But—what—is—the—matter?

Down below they are pulling the wood away from the flames. The glow dwindles; a few seconds later they have stamped out the last lingering little flame.

What does it mean? I gave orders that they were to keep it burning for at least half an hour and—the flickering reflection of a flash gleams on the varnished surface of one of our lower wings and gives me the answer—our Archie are firing. I look down and see a ring of flame belching from the mouths of cannon all around us, while over our heads the fiery balls of the shells are bursting. Now I know what has happened: a French squadron is on its way, and we poor devils are unlucky enough to have flown into the hell created by the defence.

What about it? Shall I send up a star signal to stop them firing on us?

No! That will only mean that the French machines will be allowed to go on their way unhindered. Besides, those shells are bursting fairly high above us, so that we are most unlikely to be touched by even a splinter, let alone a direct hit.

Engmann laughs and points upward. " Going after them ? " he inquires.

Of course we are going after them ! So open up your engine and full speed ahead ! I strain my eyes for a glimpse of the Frenchman, but in vain ! The dawn is still too faint—bad shooting in such a light—and, judging by the shell-bursts, the enemy must be at least 4,000 metres up. A wave of depression comes over us when we realize how hopeless are our chances ; then suddenly a bright idea comes to cheer me up.

" Too high for us," I remark. " I'm sure they're off to Charleville to tickle up our G.H.Q. a bit."

Engmann beams with delight.

" Quite healthy for the good folk there to know there's a war on," he observes.

A blow answers his disrespectful remark, but it is only a love-tap, as naturally I share his sentiments.

" Don't be so cheeky, young fellow. And as we can't catch a bird to-day, we'll play cuckoo."

Engmann fails to grasp my meaning.

" Cuckoo ? "

" Yes, cuckoo ! We'll lay our eggs in their nest."

Good old Take jogs up and down on his seat with glee. This is a business after his own heart.

" But how are we to find the aerodrome from which they started ? " he asks.

" It will be certain to be illuminated," I reassure him. He opens up his engine again.

As the twilight of early morning conceals

ourselves as well as the Frenchmen in its kindly shades, we do not need to zoom up but can fly a straight course to the front. Our impatience to play this lovely game of cuckoo will brook no long delay. But where is the right aerodrome? Where is the nest in which we must deposit our eggs?

Our tension is painfully broken by an unforeseen incident. While we are groping our way along the road from Attigny to Somme Py, a spectral arm suddenly feels its way up to us—quivers in the space around us—vanishes—quivers anew. The German motor-searchlight at Semide!

My hand feels for my light-pistol so that I can explain to him: "Look out! Friend!" But I change my mind and stick the pistol back in its hole in the floor. Let him catch us if he can. If he does, the good folk on the other side of the line will take us for one of their aeroplanes that has had to turn back for some reason and hold their fire. Besides, the early morning haze weakens the brightness of the beam so much that there is no chance of it dazzling us.

At last we reach the front. In the neighbourhood of Aubérive we fly a bare 2,000 metres over trenches cut out of chalk that forms a vivid contrast to the dark earth around it. Like white lace on black velvet.

A thrill goes through me as I gaze ahead. Where can I find an aerodrome with lighted hangars? Although my reason tells me that at this distance I cannot possibly see the tiny lights, my heart still hopes for a glimpse of them, and at last my hopes are rewarded. From the direction of Châlons a red flare gleams up to me. It darts, flickers, and dies down, reviving every now and then to cast shy, stolen glances at me. And then, halfway between it and the front I spy another light—likewise red, but constant in its dimensions.

At once I grasp the significance of these two lights. Over there where the red flare gleamed just now is the aerodrome of the French squadron. The light that is nearer to the front is there to guide the *aviateurs* on their way. Involuntarily my hand feels for the safety-catch on the bomb-rack, and I signal Engmann into the direction of the big flare.

Now it has vanished altogether. Do the starting crew guess the trouble that is coming to them?

No! Once more it glows red again—just three minutes after it had died down again. Capital! I signal Engmann to throttle back.

" St. Etienne is the aerodrome we want. That's the nest in which we are going to put our cuckoo's egg!"

Take is happy that we have found our target so quickly, and wags his head in his polar-bear rhythm. Engine full on!

Now we are approaching our objective. The red fire continues to blaze up at short intervals.

And now we are over St. Hilaire junction.

There's an Archie battery here. Hope it's not going to spoil our fun! I peer over and see a flash of light. Gunfire or some harmless light? Suspense—false alarm!

" Shut off ! "

The roar of the engine dies away ; the wind in the bracing wires is the only sound that strikes our ears.

" Glide down to the aerodrome, so that I can be sure of hitting ! "

Engmann nods and expounds his latest idea.

" I'll imitate a rotary engine."

He opens up our engine to full and then quickly throttles back again. Several times he repeats this procedure. On—off ! On—off ! On—off ! Then he makes his throttle chirp. It sounds exactly like a single-seater scout with a rotary engine preparing to land but keeping the engine on slightly so as to reduce the angle of the glide and prevent the benzine from drowning it.

I chuckle with glee. Cunning fellow—our Take !

And, lo and behold ! his trick works ! The staring crew are throwing more magnesium on their flare—to light the way for our landing !

Meanwhile we are nearly over the mark. I get the flare into my sights. The French have fed it so lavishly for the supposed *camarade's* benefit that our machine is bathed in a red glow. Rather mean of us, when you come to think of it, to reward their friendly assistance so evilly, but what else can I do ? *C'est la guerre !* Twice I pull the lever. Egg No. 1 and egg No. 2 are laid. We fly straight ahead. Now those folk down below will hear a nasty noise—and, yes, I see two big flashes, close to the red flare. I am satisfied. (See sketch at chapter heading.)

I whack Engmann into a right hand turn so that he can fly back towards the red flare. Then we repeat the process.

Ruck! ruck!

Eggs No. 3 and 4 go down. And well on the mark!

While Engmann flies off towards the front again, I turn round to look back. The blaze is not yet extinguished. *Courage, messieurs!*

We cover a goodly stretch before they get it under and stamp out the last remaining sparks. A most unpleasant surprise for them—our visit!

There seems to be something wrong with their telephone too, because we reach the front unspotted by searchlights, unshot at by Archie, unmolested by hostile aircraft.

*L'appetit vient en mangeant.* Success has not sated us; it has made us hungry for more. Once again I signal Engmann to throttle back.

"Well flown, Take. So now, sweep round to westward and we'll have another little jaunt. Before we're due south-west we shall be up to 3,000 again, which is a good thing, because the sun will soon be up. We'll do our reconnaissance job, and then let's hope that we meet the French bombers on our way home. We'll earn our bread and butter to-day!"

Twenty minutes later we cross the front line by Rheims. Although it is now almost broad daylight, the marksmanship of the French Archie is atrocious. But we bear them no ill-will on that account. On we go, over the Forêt de Rheims until

I can see Epernay. Then we turn off south-east in the direction of Châlons.

Just as Engmann turns our white bird into the new course I see that its wings are bathed in a red glow. A memory of far-away childhood awakens: I recall the ruddy glow on my grandfather's face when the Heydemarck mill was on fire. But this is only the reflection of the roseate dawn playing on our varnished wings. Dreamily I gaze out to left, where fiery swords are thrusting themselves over the horizon. How beautiful! How glorious!

The old proverb is right—not merely in the exaggerated sense of its application to lie-a-beds, but positively and literally: " Morning hours are full of gold ! "

Yes, but unfortunately they are often full of French aviators as well.

While I am still waiting for the sun's upper rim to appear, I discover a Frenchman just at the place where I thought I should find one. He must still be very far away, because I cannot make out his machine, though I see clearly enough the big red light that he fires as a signal. Presumably he is the squadron-leader of the returning bombers!

What a pity that they have turned up here, of all places! Under these conditions I have no stomach for an air fight ; I prefer to hop it. The odds of 15 to 1 twenty kilometres or so the wrong side of the front is a most unpleasing one. As the good folk will want to land at St. Etienne, I think the best thing we can do is to fly a bit farther into enemy territory and hide ourselves somewhere south of the Marne. Discretion is decidedly the better part of valour.

A very good thing that *M. le Commandeur's* lights have given us an unintentional warning in addition to directing the movements of his own squadron!

But in any case I'd better swing my machine gun round. Ready for all emergencies, then!

I put my glasses to my eyes to ascertain the enemy's numbers. The next moment I drop them again and smile as I swing my machine gun back. Venus, not Mars, is the ruler of this hour, for the light I have seen is the morning star.

A ridiculous and yet a pardonable error! At this moment Venus exceeds in magnitude and brilliancy all over stars a hundredfold because it is the hour when they fade and vanish. And why this brilliance? Because the heavenly bodies above us send down their light the shortest way through the belt of haze whereas I view the morning star horizontally, i.e., broadside on through the whole mass of the haze, which enlarges it unnaturally. The rising sun completes the illusion by tinting it red.

Engmann has noticed nothing of the comedy behind his back because he has been searching the air ahead of him for hostile aircraft. I am glad; no one wants to make a fool of himself in front of his friends. (See Illustration No. 14.)

Onward!

Not much doing to-day. Very little railway traffic about—all the hangars still shut—not a single machine in the air Because it's Sunday, perhaps? Or are they all engaged on the squadron flights?

Question! What route is the bombing squadron likely to take on its way back from Charleville? They crossed the front at Aubérive, and the wind is south-west; therefore they will probably come back via Vouziers. I am ready to bet on it.

Consequently we make for the Argonne.

The nearer we approach to the front, the more intently we search the sky for the shellbursts of the German Archie which will inform us of the squadron's approach. The French are bound to come back this way; it's a dead certainty.

But unfortunately I am a long way out in my reckoning, for just as we are worming our way through the fire put up by the Archies of Vienne-le-Château, Engmann suddenly points an excited hand to our left. Far away to westward, at a distance of quite twenty kilometres, I see a thick barrage put up by our Archie. The squadron has thus belied my logical deductions by turning round and going back the way it came. We cannot possibly reach it.

We glide down to Attigny in a depressed mood.

. . . . .

When we had landed and were getting out of our flying kit, Engmann scrutinized my face closely.

"Is the Herr Lieutenant weeping for joy at our excellent bombing work or for sorrow because the French squadron escaped us?" he inquired.

"Take" Engmann in Action

"Don't be impertinent, you silly ass. Shove me over the mirror."

When I saw my face in it, I discovered that I had caught cold in my right eye. A silent, **manly** tear welled out of one corner.

## CHAPTER XVI

### WHOSO DIGGETH A PIT FOR OTHERS . . .

I WAS slowly pulling on my fur boots when Lance-Corporal Sievers came running into the hangar.

" French squadron in the air ! "

I grabbed my glasses and ran out with the others. The shellbursts from our Archie showed us where they were looking for the Frenchmen.

" They are not visiting us to-day," I observed,

"for they're flying in the direction of Amagne and Lucquy."

So we were able to watch their further progress as there was no need to beat a shamefaced retreat to the cellar reserved for the use of heroes. Our O.C. Rockets was in a bad temper because the squadron kept its formation in spite of the peppering he gave them.

"Our Archie are sending up one shell after another," he grumbled, "and none of them is anywhere near the mark. The French are not bothering to make the slightest turning movement."

I had to laugh.

"Did you hear that, Take? We have to change our course even when the shellbursts are nowhere near us. It pleases Archie, and then they won't bother to correct their range." Quite a pleasant change to be spectators of a battle! It was the first time that the French had passed over us in broad daylight.

Engmann also waxed enthusiastic.

To think that we treat the Frenchman to this show every day for nothing! The only difference is that we don't go off in bunches of six like those fellows up there, but all on our lonesomes and fight for our lives with two, three, six, or even ten of the. . . .

We had to cease our remarks because affairs in the air above us took a dramatic turn. From the south a number of our scouts whirled up, and we could plainly see that they were gaining on their opponents both in height and distance. We watched in breathless excitement: what was going to be the issue of the fight? Now our men were close at hand; faintly we heard the "tacks" of their machine guns. A Fokker dived on to a big Frenchman—nearer—nearer—and just at the last moment he pulled his machine and jumped over the enemy. Engmann danced up and down at my side.

"What a pity he didn't get him the first go off. Or did he? Looks as if that Frenchie is going into a glide. Engine shot to pieces perhaps!"

Yes, he was right. I could plainly see the machine's nose dip. I kept the stricken opponent in the field of my glasses. And behold! from his cockpit a tiny flame shot out—the propeller wind caught it and pulled it—drawing it out into a long jet of fire behind the tail—and then the whole machine burst into flames.

Would its crew jump out with their parachutes? But apparently not all the French machines were equipped with this saving resource, and so the last act of the tragedy took place.

Glad as we were to see our own man win, the spectacle set our hearts beating wildly. We hoped that Fate would be kind enough to spare us such a fearful end. Better a bullet through the head than have your living body eaten by the flames!

The horror of the situation must have caused the observer to lose his head, or perhaps he thought: "If I must die, at least I won't die by torture in the flames!" For now a dark object emerged from the blazing machine and fell earthwards. When I focused it in my glasses, I saw that it was a human being. He spun round in the air and made desperate efforts to steer himself with his arms and legs. He was still alive—and yet we knew that in less than a minute he would be smashed to pieces on the ground. (See sketch at chapter heading.)

But the machine could not maintain its glide for long. Strapped to his seat, the pilot must already have been roasted to death by the flames that the benzine fed and the wind fanned. The burning wings detached themselves from the fuselage and fluttered through the air like a couple of butterflies, while the cockpit shot earthwards like a glowing torch.

The smoking remains fell onto a ploughed field barely a kilometre from our aerodrome. When Engmann wanted to go off with the others to see them, I held him back.

" You stay here, Take. I forbid you to go and look at it. You'd never get rid of the impression. And as it's the sort of fate that might befall us any day, you'd see those poor fellows when we were in a tight corner and had to keep our heads cool."

Engmann saw that I was right.

. . .

Later our comrades reported the details of the horrible business. The brave pilot was almost consumed by the flames. The observer who had jumped out of the burning machine from a height of 3,000 metres appeared uninjured, but when they tried to place his body on a stretcher, it was a shapeless mass which only the skin held together.

. . . . .

Five minutes later we take off to do our daily job.

Rheims—Epernay—Châlons—Ste Ménehould.

To-day there appears to be nothing important going on. But two incidents occur to annoy me.

(1) An inspection is evidently taking place a Auve aerodrome. All its sixteen machines are drawn up in neat rows of four, just as if they are on parade. And to-day of all days I am not carrying any bombs!

(2) The Archie at Fort Montbré send a shrapnel bullet through an upper wing, which passes within half a metre of my head.

As I consider every hit from an Archie as a reflection on our skill in dodging, I visit my wrath —with mankind's usual injustice—on the gunner behind the bullet and plan to incite a long-range battery of ours to make it hot for him.

"All bad things come in threes," I think.

But we fly our stretch without further mishap. With a sigh of relief I whack Engmann's left shoulder and describe a half circle with my right hand before his eyes. Then I extend my arm and point ahead to tell him: "Home again!"

But wait a minute; there's a train at Ste

## WHOSO DIGGETH A PIT FOR OTHERS

Ménehould station. I bend over to jot it down on the map.

Suddenly a violent jolt causes me to bang my head against the bomb-rack. Engmann has shut off his engine. Why?

Full of curiosity I jump up and follow the direction of his outstretched arm. Before us, to the right, a small double-decker is ploughing its aerial path. Friend or foe? From the cockpit beam-end I cannot tell at first sight, but when the machine turns off southward I see the metal of its bonnet gleam in the sunshine. A double-decker with a rotary engine—a Frenchman! And now he shows me his broadside with the red, white and blue tricolour on the fuselage.

He has not seen us yet. Well, just you wait a bit, my friend! Engmann does the smart thing by putting our machine into a line with his tail and flying after him. Bravo, Take!

" At him! " I yell in his ear.

He wriggles joyfully on his seat over the tank. A marvellous opportunity. We have never had one of those nimble little Nieuport fellows in front of our guns like this before.

Engmann releases the safety-catch from his machine gun and leans down to take aim. I feel wonderfully calm and bend over to him. But the excitement of the chase is in his blood, and to save himself trouble, he is using the larger sight. I whack his back vigorously.

" Nonsense, man! Use the other sight! And aim more ahead! "

He nods and makes a slight turn. Then he presses the trigger-button and gives the Frenchman a burst in his flank.

Tack—tack—tack—tack—tack—tack—tack...
Wonderful music!

I scream aloud with joy. The Frenchman is so completely taken by surprise that Engmann gets in at least sixty bullets on him. Then his machine dips down by the nose and plunges earthwards.

" Got him ! " flashes through my exultant heart. But suddenly he pulls his stick, evens out his machine and climbs up behind us.

My bitter disappointment at our woeful marksmanship is mingled with admiration for his brilliant display of flying. I'm sure he is an ace!

While he is swearing at the impertinence of a German two-seater—not even an *avion de chasse*!—daring to attack him, I swing my machine gun round and give him a serial fire. At the same moment he pulls his nose up until his machine is almost at right angles to the ground and gives us a series of about forty shots. Luckily for us, he is unlucky enough to miss us completely. The " tacks " of his machine gun are my only indications that he is firing.

But now he puts his machine on its nose again—whirls past us in a terrific dive—and goes into a right-hand turn that is so steeply banked that he literally stands on one wing-tip. A second later he pulls up again and pours in a hail of lead from our right.

This time his marksmanship is better. The

bullets whizz past quite close to my ears—so close that I can plainly hear their evil whistle through the roar of the engine. The next instant a bullet bangs against my hand and knocks it away from the machine gun pivot.

But I have no time now to investigate the damage. At the same moment the tough customer goes into another turn under our right wing, but this time I get him well sighted and bang a stream of bullets at him. My burst seems to have gone home, for the Nieuport goes down in a steep dive.

Hurrah!

Now I have time to look at my wounded hand. I pull my glove off. But there is only a red rip in the skin where the bullet scraped it in passing. When I examine the glove, I find only one tiny slit, as if it had been cut with a sharp knife. Bad luck for the new glove, but good luck for the old hand!

I whack Engmann and laugh at him in the mirror. He nods back, and I clap my hands with glee. " Smart bit of work " my gestures signify.

We are bound to have suffered a few hits. For a second or two those bullets were hellishly near. While Take heads for the front, I investigate.

Aha! No. 1 in the left wing! There's another; that will be No. 2! All the same, it's a good metre away from us! But No. 3 is quite near us. The bullet must have passed through the right side-flap of my seat, somewhere about the height of my knee.

Hallo! there's another on the left—just a bit lower. It looks as if we were bang in his burst!

Now where's that bullet that hit my left hand? As I look up to seek it, a strong odour of benzine strikes my nostrils. Well . . . does that mean he hit our tank?

I bend over to the pilot's seat and stare at the benzine clock. It indicates thirty litres. So the main tank is safe and sound.

And what about the little emergency tank? I look up. Yes, there's our precious fuel jetting out. The drops do not fall into the cockpit, because they are whirled away by the mighty wind of the propeller.

The next moment I notice that a tongue of flame is emitted from the exhaust with every beat of the engine.

A spark would . . .

I turn round. Cockpit and wings are dripping wet. And behind us trails the thrice accursed white banner of doom—a thick cloud of benzine gas.

One little spark could . . .

Not a second's pause between vision and action. As I turn round, I grab Engmann's arm.

" Shut off your engine ! "

The beats die down. Through the inlet valves a few drops of benzine still trickle into the cylinders —just enough to keep the pistons working and the propeller revolving. Engmann turns a questioning face towards me.

" Emergency tank holed ! "

He looks up and nods.

" Shall I cut off the ignition ? " he asks.

I consider. If that brings the propeller and the engine to a standstill, we shall have to land just where we can. But better that than roast up here at 3,000 and come down a glowing mass as that poor Caudron did this morning.

" Cut off ignition ! " I order.

Engmann bends down to his left.

" Magnetos 1 and 2—off ! "

Down go the contact breakers with a sharp snap. The propeller makes a couple of tired revs., and the pistons rise and fall ever slower and slower.

Blubb ! Blurrubb ! Blubb !

Engine and propeller cease work. Engmann's hand expresses a gesture of regret, and I shrug my shoulders. What a pity ! If the emergency tank had run dry and the benzine in the cockpit had evaporated, we could have flown on without any risk. Up here we shall never get the engine going again—we are dead sure about that. Never mind ! If we have to make an emergency landing, we shan't lose anything except our time.

The main thing is that we shan't be burnt to death.

All this has happened so quickly. Scarcely fifteen seconds have passed since the moment when I fired my last shot at the Frenchman . . . The Frenchman——

I turn round at lightning speed. But he is nowhere to be seen, and there are no other aeroplanes about.

That is a blessing; if a phosphorus bullet pierced our benzine-drenched cockpit, it would be ... well, another story!

I stare in front of me. The altimeter shows 2,800. We shall clear the front easily. Below us I can see the French reserve positions, and already the Archie are giving us a lavish dose of shells and shrapnels. And now we are far enough on to land somewhere out of range of the French artillery. Topping!

2,500.

If there was no wind, we could glide twelve kilometres from such a height. With to-day's wind against us we can manage about ten.

2,200.

As the speed of our glide is slow, I get a splash of benzine in my face every time that a gust hits us or Engmann dodges a shell burst by a turn. Can I possibly patch up the holes in the tank?

Hastily I grab a few scraps of oakum from my pocket and wind them round the business end of the screwdriver. Then I try to ram this improvised stopper into a hole. It seems to work, but when I gingerly withdraw my screwdriver, the oakum comes away with it, and a lusty jet of benzine smacks me in the face. The next moment the rush of air has reduced it to vapour. I feel it freeze on my skin, and the glass of my goggles is coated with ice. I push them up on to my forehead and try again.

1,800.

Time is pressing. Luckily we are now out of

range of Archie, so that I can work in peace.

I withdraw my screwdriver very slowly and cautiously this time, and the oakum wad remains behind in the hole. Engmann looks up and rejoices with me.

"Try if you can get the engine going again! A nose-dive might do the trick!"

He nods and switches the contact breakers off. Then he pushes the stick over and goes down with all the bracing wires howling and whistling. I feel as if my heart and stomach were forcing their way up into my throat and hold on to the struts of the centre section with both hands.

Engmann turns the handle at lightning speed.

Nothing happens!

He tries again.

Still nothing happens. The propeller does not move a hair's-breadth. The engine remains dead.

Engmann shrugs his shoulders and puts the machine into its normal glide again.

1,200.

The nose-dive has eaten up several hundred metres of our height. While I look out for a suitable landing-place I become conscious of a strong smell of benzine again. Engmann has to bend his head over to keep the stuff out of his eyes. It pours on to my helmet and leather jacket, burns my eyes and then turns to ice on my face and hands.

As soon as I recover my power of vision, I examine the tank once more. There is a wide crack between the two holes I stopped, and further investigations reveal a third hole that I had overlooked.

I pull the plug out again so that the wind can catch the benzine and carry it away behind us. This, at least, will stop it spouting into Engmann's face. There is no further danger of the machine catching fire as the ignition is switched off.

900.

Time to think about a landing-place. In what direction is the ground-wind blowing? I bend over to Engmann again.

"Do you see the smoke of an engine coming up from that open space?" I ask. "That shows the wind's due south!"

While Engmann searches the landscape for a stretch of level ground, I see something that sends an exultant thrill through my veins.

"That village down there is Monthois!" I shout. "Over there, to the right of the haystacks, is the old aerodrome. That's where we'll land!"

400.

Now we are on velvet. Our troubles all over. We can make a forced landing down there—wait till all the benzine is out of the emergency tank—then I'll swing the propeller—and we'll get home on the thirty litres there still are in the main tank. A left-hand turn brings us against the wind and towards our landing-place. Hurriedly I snatch the two ends of my belt and buckle them round my body. Best be ready for emergencies! If we turn turtle I might otherwise be shot out over the machine's nose—which would be a splendid opportunity to break my neck—in spite of my hard head and my crash helmet.

Our white bird descends in a graceful glide. Now the wheels are touching the ground—but just at that moment the shock of landing sends a vigorous jet of benzine into Engmann's eyes—he is blinded—cannot see the little rise in the ground that lies in our path—bumpety bump! we run into it—and the way that is still on our machine bounces her into the air again.

Quick as lightning it flashes through my brain: " Bad luck. Now we're in for a nasty crash!"

We come down like a log of wood—sideslip over the right wing—" ratch!" say the spars and ribs of the right wing as they splinter—" rountz " says the undercarriage as it cracks off—" zuck!" says the machine as she goes over on to her nose—my hands grip the sides of the cockpit—and the next moment we have turned turtle! (See Illustration No. 15.)

Like a weasel, I creep out of the debris. No need to unbuckle my safety-belt. The shock of the crash has torn it apart.

" Take ? "

Laboriously he worms his way out of the pilot's seat. His safety belt has likewise gone to pieces and the shock pitched him against the upper rim of the windscreen. With his handkerchief he tries to staunch the blood running from his mouth and nose, as we silently survey our dead bird.

" Bad luck, Take! I was so bucked at the idea that we would be able to fly home all right!"

Engmann is depressed. "I put her down so beautifully," he says, "and then I got that damned benzine in my eyes!"

Once again he wipes away the oozing blood with his handkerchief. I try to console him.

"Well, it doesn't matter now! And we had the devil's own luck in our scrap. Just look here—seven hits! Those three in the emergency tank must have passed right between the pair of us. Look at that big hole up there—you could almost get your hand in it. A jolly good thing it wasn't an incendiary bullet!"

But Engmann can conjure up no pleasure at the thought of our victory in the air, for he is still mourning over our machine.

"I'll have a squint at the damage!" he says.

Unfortunately it is severe. The main spar and all ribs of the right upper wing are broken, and the undercarriage can be completely written off. The propeller is a mass of splinters, the exhaust and radiator are bent, while the cockpit is split right across.

Our lovely machine! Machine? No, for us it was no dead piece of machinery but a living creature. We loved our old " griffin " as tenderly as any cavalryman loves his horse. Her graceful form, when we approached the aerodrome—her excellent climb when we started off—her speed when she flew us over the front—her lithe movements when we snaked our way through the Archie—her agility when we had to get out of an opponent's burst in a fight—the song of her bracing wires when we came back over the front

Our forced Landing after a Fight in the Air

once more—the honourable scars of her bullet holes ringed round with red and black circles—all these things we loved in her.

And now, with a smile of forgiveness, we remembered her faults, her vices and her tricks—how she never liked carrying bombs—how she tried to turn turtle in the clouds—how she never would turn about properly in an air-fight—how she went on strike when we were flying over Châlons—how she refused to let go of the eggs we wanted to drop.

And now our good old " griffin " is dead !

And then *la bête humaine,* the beast in mankind, breaks loose in my soul. " Rather she than we ! " I think.

Then I turn to Engmann, who stands at my side, lost in his meditations. " All pretty well washed out except the engine," I comment. " That seems more or less O.K. Ought to be worth something ! "

Engmann nods gloomily.

" She'll have to be scrapped ! "

I give him a friendly nudge in the ribs.

" Sometimes you've simply marvellous observation faculties, young fellow ! I thought we'd be able to start off again in a few minutes ! "

Meanwhile soldiers come running up.

" Where's the nearest telephone ? " I inquire.

" Over there, in the village, Herr Lieutenant ! "

Five minutes later I get on to our squadron-leader. I give him a brief report of our reconnaissance and fight in the air. He is pleased to hear that all has gone off so well.

"I'll send the works sergeant along to you with a car and two lorries with a dismantling squad. So long . . . au revoir."

I sit down on the grass beside Engmann, and we both stare at our dead bird. Suddenly we prick up our ears. From the northward air the miaowing of bursting shrapnels and the roar of shell fire reaches our ears. And soon afterwards our naked eyes can count the enemy machines . . . eleven of them . . . a French bombing squadron on its way home.

And at their heels is a swarm of German scouts.

Tack—tack—tack—tack—tack . . .

And we are helpless . . . earthbound . . . envying our more fortunate comrades.

"Bad luck!"

Engmann nods.

"Awful!"

Then I laugh at him.

"As far as to-day's concerned, it is. To-morrow we'll get a new bird out of the park. And then what ho, Take!"

## CHAPTER XVII

### I HAD A COMRADE . . .

ORIGINALLY I planned to take my leave as soon as Take Engmann came back from his. But something always turned up to stop me—I had to teach a new photographic officer his job—then things seemed to be getting lively round Verdun way—and then I wanted to make sure that good old Take got his E.K.1[1]

"Orders and distinctions" were a chapter apart —generally speaking and also as conversational topic No. 9 in the mess. We did not measure their real value by the fact that we got them; the important thing that mattered was—how and why we got them. I was proud of my cross because my brigadier, who had his given to him on the same day, would not put it on at once. "I can't wear it," he said to General Litzmann, "until my adjutant is back from his job and can put his on too."

There was a good "why" for Engmann's cross. When Captain Drechsel submitted his name for it, the chief of the general staff said in amazement: "What? Hasn't he got it yet?"

[1] Iron Cross (Eisernes Kreuz), 1st class.—TRANSLATOR'S NOTE.

He made a mark against his name, which meant much.

. . . . .

When this last obstacle to my departure was removed, I was able to buzz off home. I was glad to be off, as I felt very played out. In the long run flying over the enemy's lines day in and day out plays havoc with one's nerves, loathe as I am to admit it. We did not often have a "walk-over" when we went reconnoitring round Châlons way, for as the autumn days were drawing shorter, flying activities were concentrated into fewer hours, and consequently our losses increased. From our unit of twelve men that worked six two-seaters (which was brought up to strength again after every casualty) we suffered the following losses within the space of ten months: 4 slightly wounded, 6 severely wounded, 4 taken prisoners, 6 killed.

I was therefore glad of a chance to be out of harness for awhile.

. . . . .

Engmann accompanied me to the station. Just before the train went off I leant out of the window and talked to him. I saw that he was sorry to lose me for a while and knew that his regrets were sincere from my own experience. I had felt just the same when he went off on leave. I tried to console him.

"Take, old fellow, you know what Lieutenant Holzhausen is always saying: 'Hold your head up, cock your chin and cross your thumbs, and then your horse will trot!' besides, as winter is coming on, you'll have lots of rain and clouds, which means there won't be much flying. You'll see how the time will go! And when I'm back again, we'll do our incendiary bomb show at Mourmelon camp, and after that we'll have a go at the munition dump south of the Marne."

At these pleasing prospects Engmann brightened up a bit.

"At any rate, I'll be glad when we're together again."

A last hand grip, and then my train passed out into the night.

. . . .

When on my last day of leave I returned to Attigny station, I looked round for Engmann. A pilot gave me the news.

"Severely wounded to-day!"

My dear old Take!

Engmann had gone out with a new observer. (See Illustration No. 16.) He had had a fight with three Nieuports and was shot through the lungs, but brought his machine back across the lines and made an emergency landing. Then he was carried off unconscious to the hospital at Bétheniville.

As everyone knew how dear Take was to me, my first evening meal in the mess was a silent affair. The way in which my comrades showed their sympathies did me good.

There was other bad news.

Lieutenant Gerstenberger (observer): shell-shock, following a direct hit on the machine's wing.

Officer's-substitute Scheidt (pilot): severely wounded in an air-fight.

Lieutenant Fritsche (observer): shot through the head in an air-fight; dead.

Captain Linke (pilot) and Lieutenant Steinbrenner (observer), who had been shortly before transferred to a fighting squadron: shot down on a close reconnaissance: both dead.

Captain Elias tried to console me for my personal loss.

" Until your Take is on his legs again, I'll give you Diessner for your pilot. He's the best of our new lot. I'm sure that in a little while you'll have taught him his job as thoroughly as you taught our good Engmann."

I smiled sadly. Six months or even a year might elapse before my friend's lungs were healed again. I had no desire to stay all that time in a squadron where everything reminded me of him, and was therefore glad that my former chief, Captain Mohr, had kept his promise and put in an application for my transfer to his new squadron, No. 30, which was attached to the 1st Bulgarian Army Corps. I felt that I could no longer do good work with No. 17.

Here my so-called " luck " on every flight was solely due to my oneness with my brother-in-arms, Take. Now that I was compelled to lack his company for such a long time I knew that he and

16 ENGMANN (LEFT) BEFORE HIS LAST FLIGHT

*Facing page 206*

I were a unit; without him I was only a half. In Macedonia, on a new front, associated with new comrades against a new foe—I should not feel myself so oppressed by his absence as here. Out there I should soon be my old self again.

That same evening I got the hospital on the telephone.

"Crisis not yet over!" was the report.

. . . .

Captain Elias had put a car at my disposal for the next day. But I could make no use of it, for when I rang up again, the news was gloomy.

"Patient's condition worse. We'll let you know!"

. .

That afternoon I went to see Engmann's machine, which had been dismantled and brought back to Attigny. Riddled with shots and damaged by the forced landing, it seemed to me to be a fitting memorial to my comrade.

My restlessness would not let me stay at the aerodrome. As it was impossible for any machine to start out in the drizzle, I wandered sorrowfully along the towpath of the canal that I had so often trod with Take.

Not until the twilight fell did I return Attigny.

The report was there.

. . . dead . . .

**THE END**

www.ingramcontent.com/pod-product-compliance
Lightning Source LLC
Chambersburg PA
CBHW070841160426
43192CB00012B/2263